WELCOMING HOME BABY

the Handcrafted Way

20 Quick & Creative Knitted Hats, Wraps & Cozy Cocoons for Your Newborn

TRICIA DRAKE

Photography by Brooke Kelly

SELLERS
PUBLISHING

DEDICATION

This book is dedicated to my wonderful husband, Timothy, who single-handedly and selflessly kept our busy household afloat while I did nothing but knit and write for months; and to our seven sweet and happy children: Will Mason, Bella, Lissa Clare, Matthew, Alex, Max, and baby Jeannie — you make my life a party of nine every day.

CONTENTS

INTRODUCTION

Like so many knitters out there, I have been a knitting "dabbler" off and on since my grandmother taught me to knit when I was a teenager. I have been through countless crafting cycles that have alternated between periods of being consumed with knitting fever — when my needles would burn like a comet for a few months and I would knit anything and everything in my path — and periods of relative yarnlessness that for whatever reason would often turn into months of knitting hiatus as my crafting obsession gravitated to other handwork (needle felting runs a close second to knitting for me).

It was during one of these upswings in my knitting biorhythm several years ago when I decided I wanted to knit some cute hats for my children — something funky and unique. Heaven knows I had plenty of yarn (just ask my husband) and plenty of children (again, just ask my husband — we had six at that time, seven now), but I lacked a critical ingredient — TIME. Six children under eight years old meant I had absolutely no time to devote to what I assumed would only be a laborious task. I was lamenting about this dilemma to my sister, who shot me a puzzled look and said, "Why is it you can make a long scarf in 30 minutes, but not a tiny hat?"

It was a huge "Aha!" moment.

I had been knitting with beautiful bulky yarns on big needles (strictly 19s and above) for years because I liked the speedy results and interesting textures, so why couldn't I knit a baby hat the way I knit everything else? What was stopping me, other than the long-accepted, unwritten rule that small items for small people must be knit on small needles using small (i.e., fine) yarn? Once I unshackled myself from that conventional ball and chain, I became an unstoppable knitting machine. I was off to the races (my local yarn store) at a dizzying two stitches to the inch and haven't looked back since.

A few weeks later, I was shopping with my children. I was sporting one of my own scarves and two of my children were wearing hats I had whipped up. The owner of the shop asked if I wanted to make a few pieces to put in her boutique. Turns out they sold like hotcakes and I was quickly filling more orders. Shortly after, I started my own business, TrickyKnits, and started selling unusual scarves, chunky baby hats, and cozy newborn cocoons online. A photographer that I had met asked if I would design a line of handknit props — cocoons, pods, wraps, hats, hammocks, etc., — for her to use in her newborn shoots. Her beautiful images led to more exposure among other photographers, and my business has continued to expand.

The 20 projects in this book include many of my most popular designs — colorful and happy little knits for new parents, newborn photographers, or anyone welcoming a wee one into their lives. Some I created with special occasions in mind — sweet hats for bringing baby home from the hospital, delicate wraps for celebratory first introductions, cozy cocoons for tender newborn photographs — and others are suited for more everyday use. I hope you find all of the patterns to be creative and whimsical projects you can count on to delight the recipient, whether you're in a bind for a quick baby shower gift or are creating a family heirloom.

Many of the projects are easily completed in a couple of hours (and likely less, once you get the hang of them). Quite a few are small enough to fit right into your purse — or certainly a hip and jaunty knitting project bag (which you rightly deserve and should own). And because I love creating new variations of patterns to suit my mood (or my recipient's taste), and I can't always dash right out to my local yarn store for a specific yarn, I've given you suggestions of different colorways or other yarns for all of the patterns, to give you an idea of how broadly you can interpret them and make something truly one-of-a-kind.

These are your patterns now, so bring a piece of yourself to them. Go ahead! Knit. Create. Enjoy.

www.trickyknits.com

TIPS FROM TRICKYKNITS

I have put together this collection of patterns to appeal to any knitter, regardless of skill level. That being said, I am going to assume that you already know the basics of knitting — or if you don't, you are enough enthused by this book to take a class, corner a friend, or spend some time on the Internet learning how to cast on, knit, purl, bind off, and pick up stitches. The videos on knittinghelp.com are a valuable resource. For all of the other stitches and techniques used in these patterns (e.g., decreasing, increasing), I've included instructions to guide you through the process. I've tried to write these patterns as if I were right there with you, and I've pointed out places where it might be easy to make a mistake if you're not paying attention.

The abbreviations I've used are the standards accepted by the Craft Yarn Council. Once you become familiar with them, you will be able to read any knitting pattern. I've also provided both the U.S. and metric sizing for needles (and the occasional crochet hook used in these patterns.

Yarn, Knitting Needles, and Other Supplies

YARN

A richly spun yarn, like a spray-on tan, will hide a multitude of sins. That's why I like working with them. A little gaff in the middle of a row of stockinette knit up in a worsted weight on say, size 7s, will rudely point at you and relentlessly guffaw until you, defeated and browbeaten, rip out all those hundreds of stitches to quell it. That same snafu whipped up with a textured handspun on 19s will just wink with a wry "don't worry — it's all good" smile and never make another peep. If a pattern starts out "With size 8s and a worsted weight yarn, cast on 200 stitches" — ughhh, I tell you I am already turning the page. I would never even cast on a project — forget finishing one. But not my friend, Pamela. She is a sock knitter (the saintliest of all knitters, if you ask me). Patient, dear Pamela knit a beautiful baby blanket for me when my seventh child, Jeannie, was born in 2009. It was an intricate design, knit in a dainty worsted with hundreds of rows, countless exquisite bobbles, and deftly slipped stitches — a sweet little pattern that looked like an endless number of children (reminiscent of my own) holding hands. I burst into tears when I opened it because I instantly felt the weight of the many hours Pamela must have spent toiling away on it. As I admired her handiwork, running my fingers over each tiny, perfect stitch, she recounted how she had started it in December when she found out I was pregnant, worked on it every spare moment she could find, and managed to finish it the morning we brought Jeannie home from the hospital in July.

WHAT?! Did I just hear that right? Seven months to make this? Are you kidding me?!

Through my tears I confessed to her right at that moment that she would never, ever be receiving anything like that from me. Why? Because I'm too smitten with chunky yarn, how it gallops over and under your needles, quickly serving up row after row of juicy contentedness until the next thing you know, you've just whipped up a hat. Not that worsteds and the like don't have their place – I've gleefully knit with beautiful worsteds (there are actually a few choice ones in this book) - but my heart lies with the bulky weights simply because I am an impatient knitter. I'm not a *lazy* knitter, mind you – I will begrudgingly take time to gauge when necessary, I (usually) take time to wind my hanks into a ball instead of recklessly trying to knit from them – but the bottom line is I like quick results. With seven young children in my hair, I want (and deserve) instant knitting rapture. Big yarns knit on big needles provide such rapture.

With so many delicious yarns available today, it is often hard to decide which will best suit a pattern. I generally prefer natural fibers, such as wool, cotton, silk, mohair, and blends of these, over synthetics such as acrylic and polyester. I do love a fun novelty yarn as an accent (this is almost always some kind of synthetic blend), but I usually use a merino wool or organic cotton as the main yarn in my pieces. Both are wonderfully soft against baby's sensitive skin and provide excellent breathability and wearability for items meant for everyday use. In this book, I've purposefully used a wide variety of yarns — and referenced many others as alternatives — to encourage you to think outside the box when designing your own versions of these pieces. My advice is to keep baby's comfort in mind and use the highest-quality yarn you can afford. After all, you are knitting a treasure!

When selecting yarns for your project, be sure to purchase enough of the same dye lot (check the label!). Yarn is dyed in limited quantities and the variation between the lots can sometimes be enough to bring woe and despair upon the unsuspecting knitter.

The yarn label will also indicate how to care for items made from that yarn. Be sure to follow those instructions, and if you are gifting your little handknit, take a moment to write the fiber content and care instructions on a notecard for your recipient. Take it from me, most handknits don't take kindly to wringing, twisting, or extreme water temperatures. I hand-wash my items with Soak™, a no-rinse, biode-gradable liquid soap especially formulated for delicate items.

Knitting Needle Sizes	
Metric (mm)	U.S.
2.0	0
2.25	1
2.75	2
3.0	-
3.25	3
3.5	4
3.75	5
4.0	6
4.5	7
5.0	8
5.5	9
6.0	10
6.5	10.5
7.0	-
7.5	-
8.0	11
9.0	13
10.0	15
12.75	17
15.0	19
19.0	35
25.0	50

courtesy of the Craft Yarn Council, Gastonia, N.C.

Be aware that some of the projects in this collection were designed for special occasions or limited wear and call for delicate yarns, or even a length of elegant silk ribbon. These items require extra attention in their care. Some hand-dyed silk ribbon available in specialty stores is not colorfast, so be sure to either use colorfast ribbon or have your piece dry-cleaned.

Finally, I must now say a brief word about the materials I used for making the items shown in this book: all good things must come to an end, including beautiful yarns. The yarn gods seem to relish discontinuing some of our favorites, but luckily they are constantly delighting us with even more tantalizing offerings - sort of the knitter's circle of life. I'm always on the hunt for new yarns (especially of the chunky variety) and will periodically send out announcements of new findings in the TrickyKnits e-newsletter (subscribe at www.TrickyKnits.com). If you're having trouble tracking down a particular yarn in this book, consider looking around on the knitting website Ravelry at www.ravelry.com/designers/tricia-drake to see what other knitters are using for these projects, or contact me through the TrickyKnits Web site.

NEEDLES

Knitting needles come in a dizzying assortment of types, materials, and sizes. There are straight, circular, or double-pointed needles in various lengths and diameters. You can choose from metal (usually coated aluminum or brass), plastic, or wood. I won't go into detail describing the differences or the uses for each type, as that information is available in any beginning knitting book and on the Internet. I will tell you that after scouring the land for the perfect circulars, I was inspired to develop my own line of TrickyKnits needles. They're hand-crafted from fine bamboo and feature an innovative tubing connector so your stitches glide effortlessly from needle to tubing to needle. They're silent to use (important when knitting in bed or while holding a sleeping infant), warm to the touch, and much lighter than metal. No more fighting your stitches back on the needle from a skimpy piece of plastic wire. Besides, I love the notion of using something handmade to create my own handmade items. But I have also used Lion Brand plastic needles (straights and circulars) in large sizes for years and still find them perfectly suitable.

When it comes to needle sizes, I rarely knit on anything smaller than 17s. (That being said, I have to admit that while designing the pieces for this book I was so smitten with a couple of tantalizing lighter-weight yarns that I betrayed my own mantra — I picked up some 10s for the sake of supreme cuteness, and I think the payoff was worth it indeed.) I know many of you may not even own 17s, much less 19s, but I ask that you take the plunge and see for yourself all the goodness they hold. Trust me — freeing yourself from the convention that baby items must be knit on teeny needles (I don't even own any) with finely gauged stitchwork opens up a whole new world of possibilities to yourself and, more important, to all the little bodies in your life. It's like having a knitting superpower to fast-forward a project.

The needles used for projects in this book are US 19, 17, 15, and 10 straights and circulars (you can knit everything — even the flat patterns — on circulars if you prefer and not even worry about tracking down straights); and US 17 and 15 double-pointed needles. I also use a size J crochet hook for the crocheted embellishments on a couple of projects. The straights and circulars in these sizes are available at craft stores and your local yarn shop; for the double-pointeds, you will almost certainly have to purchase them at a yarn shop or order them online.

I have used a wide variety of larger sizes to allow you to wade into these waters a bit at a time. If you are new to using bigger needles and feel most comfortable in the size 3-9 range, then start out with the Party on Your Head hat, which is knit on 10s. You can work your way up to such pieces as the Tab Top Cocoon and the Ho Ho Ho! Cocoon, which are both knit on 15s, then progress to the projects on 17s and 19s.

SUPPLIES

If you have your yarn and needles, you're almost ready to begin! Here are a few other items to have on hand:

Yarn needles are enormous sewing needles with a big eye for easily threading yarn. They're quite handy for sewing up seams, weaving in any untidy ends, sewing on pom-poms, etc. Buy several, as they are notorious for escaping. **Stitch markers** are usually little plastic rings that fit on your needle between your stitches, or sometimes are attached to your fabric. Think of them as mile markers that show you the lay of the land in your piece. They are a must for knitting in the round. Sadly, it is hard to find stitch markers in big sizes, so don't spend too much time looking. Just tie a short scrap of contrasting yarn in a circle and slide it onto your needle. **Stitch holders** are used to corral live stitches so you can work on them later. **Safety pins** or **straight pins** are good to have around when your seams need to be reminded of their proper place as you are trying to sew them. Pick up the rust-proof variety if you plan to do any steaming or wet-blocking of your finished pieces. You'll want to have a **tape measure** or **short ruler** to measure the size of your piece. Also helpful are a **notebook** and **pencil** for keeping track of your progress in a pattern or jotting down a brilliant idea. A really good pair of **scissors** — above all else! — will save your hands from yarn burns, and your teeth from bits of wispy fiber. Need I say more?

How to Crochet an Embellishment

If you are looking for a way to add a little flourish to your finished handknits, consider a simple crocheted embellishment. It's easy to do, completely transforms your knitted piece, and better still, is easy to undo if you change your mind. Just pull it out and start over!

Begin with your knitted item (stockinette stitch provides a nice, smooth canvas), a contrasting yarn, and a crochet hook. (The size of the hook isn't important as long as it can fit through the knitting, grab the yarn, and pass back through the knitting without leaving an irreparable exit wound.)

Photo 1: Hold your contrasting yarn at the back/wrong side of your piece. Pass your crochet hook through the front side to the back and loop your yarn around the hook, leaving a tail long enough to weave in later.

Photo 2: Draw the hook with the loop of contrasting yarn through to the right side of the fabric.

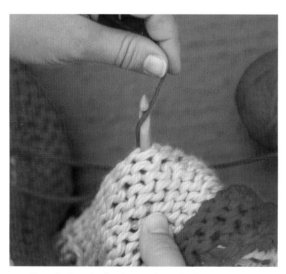

Photo 3: Keep the first loop on the neck of the crochet hook and pass the hook through to the back of the fabric (in whichever direction you want your design to travel). Wrap another loop of contrasting yarn around the hook.

Photo 4: Pull the hook to the front again and you'll have TWO (2) loops on your hook.

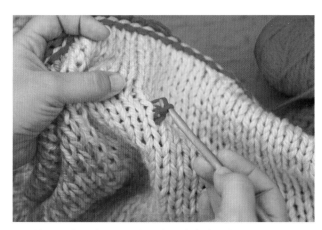

Photo 5: Draw the second loop through the first, leaving ONE (1) loop on your hook. This is your first stitch of crocheted embellishment.

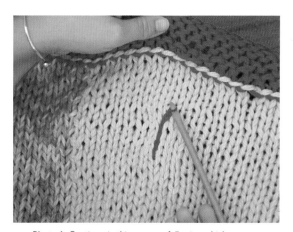

Photo 6: Continue in this manner, following whichever direction your fancy takes you. I like to think of it as doodling on my knitting because it is so easy to try a freehand design. If you don't like what you've done, remove the crochet hook and pull the working end of the yarn to undo your stitches. To finish, cut your yarn and pull the tail yarn to the front of the fabric through the last loop, and back through to the wrong side of your work. Weave in your ends.

Photo 7: The finished embellishment on the Later Gator Blanket.

How to Sew a Mattress Stitch

This very simple technique is used to join two pieces together when the stitches are running the same direction on both pieces. The mattress stitch creates an invisible seam, so you don't necessarily have to use the same yarn as your knitting. It is done along the edge (or selvage) stitches on the right side of the pieces you are seaming, so it has the double advantage of making it easy to match a pattern across the seam, as well as disguising the often disobedient edges that occur along stockinette stitch.

Photo 1: Lay your pieces side by side with the right sides up. Thread a yarn needle with new yarn (or the tail yarn, if it is long enough). Insert needle into the lowest corner stitch of one piece, and then the other piece, from back to front. Pull to close the gap. Gently separate the edge stitches and insert your needle under the horizontal bar between the first stitch and the stitch above it and draw the yarn through (it doesn't have to be pulled tightly yet).

Photo 2: Locate the horizontal bar between the stitches directly opposite on the other piece and insert your needle under that bar. Draw the yarn through. Continue back and forth, inserting the needle under the bar on one piece then on the opposite piece, until you've worked a few rows.

Photos 3 and 4: Gently tug on both ends of your yarn. Your pieces will miraculously begin to cozy up next to each other with no sign at all of the seaming yarn. Continue until you reach the end of the seam, adjusting your tension along the way so that the seam lies flat. Finish by drawing your needle through the last two corner stitches as you did for the first two in the lower edge. Weave in the remaining yarn on the wrong side.

How to Make a Pom-Pom

Pom-poms add such a fun finishing touch to just about any project and are a great way to use up little oddments of yarn in your stash. I like to use a plastic pom-pom maker (available in many sizes at any craft store), but those handy gadgets seem to disappear in my house. Fortunately, cardboard circles work just as well.

Photo 1: Cut 2 identical circles out of a piece of cardboard (a cereal box works nicely) slightly larger than the size you want the pom-pom to be, then cut a hole in the center of each circle, creating a notch or "C" shape. Hold the circles together and wrap yarn around the circles. The more yarn you wrap, the fuller your pom-pom will be.

Photo 2: Slide your scissors between the pieces of cardboard and cut the yarn all the way around the circles.

Photo 3: Before you remove the cardboard circles, gently separate them and tie a length of yarn around the bundle of yarn between the circles. Be sure to knot it tightly!

Photo 4: Remove the cardboard and fluff your beautiful pom-pom, trimming any ends as necessary.

HATS

Keep those noggins toasty!

Sweet Dreams Hat

Dashing through the Snow Hat

Chinny Chin Chinstrap Cap

Party on Your Head Hat

Criss-Cross Hat

Twisted Taffy Hat

Chunky Beanie

SWEET DREAMS HAT

This dreamy little number is such a showstopper on teeny noggins. The fluffy nubs of this *Pixie Dust* yarn look like colorful little clouds dancing around their heads. Whipped up on 17s, the newborn size is just 12 rounds of 20 stitches and no seaming — great when you're late for the shower and still don't have a gift. I've actually knit one up in the car while a friend drove us to the party — shhhh!

Skills Required: Knitting in the round on double-pointed needles, 3-needle bind-off

Size: Fits newborn/head size up to 14" (3–6 months/head size up to 17"; 6–12 months/head size up to 19")

Gauge: 8 sts and 11 rows = 4"/10cm over St st

Notes: This hat is knit in the round on double-pointed needles, then bound off across the top using the 3-needle technique. I've given a brief tutorial of this very simple technique at the end of this pattern.

Glossary of Abbreviations

BO	bind off
CC	contrasting color
CO	cast on
MC	main color
st(s)	stitch(es)
St st	stockinette stitch

* repeat instructions following the asterisk as directed

Materials

- 1 skein Cascade *Magnum* in #9551 Lemondrop (for yellow/green) (123yd/112m - 8.8oz/250g; 100% wool) or 1 hank Blue Sky Alpacas *Bulky* in #1218 Azalea (for azalea/orange) (45yd/41m - 3.5oz/100g; 50% alpaca/50% wool) (MC)

- 1 skein Knit Collage *Pixie Dust* in Kiwi Twinkle (for yellow/green) or Mango Glitter (for azalea/orange) (35yd/32m - 5oz/145g; 55% wool/40% mohair/5% camel fiber) (CC) — you really only need about 2yd per hat

- US 17 (12.75mm) double-pointed needles

- Stitch marker or scrap yarn

- Tape measure

- Scissors

A vibrant, captivating duo — Blue Sky Alpacas Bulky in Azalea (MC) snuggled around Knit Collage Pixie Dust in Mango Glitter (CC).

A soft, delicious combination — Cascade Magnum in Lemondrop (MC) wrapped around Knit Collage Pixie Dust in Kiwi Twinkle (CC).

Happy baby Presley sports the 3–6 month Sweet Dreams Hat in Lime.

Knitting the Sweet Dreams Hat

This sweet hat is knit in the round on double-pointed needles. I prefer to carry the CC up the inside of the hat for the few rows I use the MC between the stripes of CC, but you can cut the CC and pick it up again if you prefer. I have written out each st in each round, but if you are experienced enough to recognize the difference between a knit and purl st in your piece, then it will be useful for you to know that for all work done in the MC, you will knit the knit sts, and purl the purl sts to create the columns of sts on the hat. Note that this hat has no seaming and no decreasing — it is a chunky square finished with a 3-needle bind-off across the top. What could be easier?

Begin with US 17 (12.75mm) double-pointed needles and MC. After you CO your appropriate number of sts, place marker and join to work in the round, taking care not to twist sts.

FOR NEWBORN SIZE, CO 20 STS:

Rounds 1–3: With MC, *knit 2, purl 2. Repeat from * to end of round.

Round 4: Drop, but do not cut MC. With CC, knit.

Rounds 5–8: Repeat Rounds 1–4.

Rounds 9–12: Cut CC and with MC, repeat Round 1.

BO using 3-needle technique, as directed on page 25. Weave in all ends. Pull chunky nubs of CC through to the outside of your hat.

FOR 3–6 MONTH SIZE, CO 24 STS:

Rounds 1–4: With MC, knit 3, purl 2, knit 2, purl 2, knit 3, purl 3, knit 2, purl 2, knit 2, purl 3.

Round 5: Drop, but do not cut MC. With CC, knit.

Rounds 6–10: Repeat Rounds 1–5.

Rounds 11–17: Cut CC and with MC, repeat Round 1.

BO using 3-needle technique, as directed on page 25. Weave in all ends. Pull chunky nubs of CC through to the outside of your hat.

FOR 6–12 MONTH SIZE, CO 28 STS:

Rounds 1–5: With MC, knit 3, purl 3, knit 2, purl 3, knit 3, purl 3, knit 3, purl 2, knit 3, purl 3.

Round 6: Drop, but do not cut MC. With CC, knit.

Rounds 7–12: Repeat Rounds 1–6.

Rounds 13–19: Cut CC and with MC, repeat Round 1.

BO using 3-needle technique, as directed on page 25. Weave in all ends. Pull chunky nubs of CC through to the outside of your hat.

Variations

One of my favorite things about this pattern is its versatility. You can totally change the look by adding pom-poms, tassels, or tiny bows at the corners. You could even try binding off with your accent yarn to create a whimsical little row of fun across the top of the hat. And don't limit yourself to the ultra-chunky and funky yarns I've used here — try using two or more strands of something finer held together as the main yarn. If you've found an interesting accent yarn that isn't quite as bulky as *Pixie Dust* you can always double- or triple-strand that yarn to make up for one super-chunky yarn like *Pixie Dust* and still maintain the correct height of your hat.

Fun hats in a row! From left to right are the 3–6 month size in pale blue Frost and zesty Lime, and newborn size in cheery Lemondrop and brilliant Azalea.

YARN / AGE VARIATIONS

(newborn size materials on p. 21)

3–6 MONTH SIZE IN PALE BLUE:

- 1 hank Blue Sky Alpacas *Bulky* in #1211 Frost (45yd/41m - 3.5oz/100g; 50% alpaca/50% wool) (MC)

- 1 skein Knit Collage *Pixie Dust* in Kiwi Twinkle (35yd/32m - 5oz/145g; 55% wool/40% mohair/5% camel fiber) (CC) — you need about 2yd per hat

3–6 MONTH SIZE IN LIME GREEN:

- 1 skein Cascade *Magnum* in #9481 Lime (123yd/112m - 8.8oz/250g;100% wool) (MC)

- 1 skein Knit Collage *Pixie Dust* in Cerulean (35yd/32m - 5oz/145g; 55% wool/40% mohair/5% camel fiber) (CC) — you need about 2yd per hat

3-Needle Bind-off

This technique is much simpler than it may sound. In fact, if you can bind off with 2 needles (i.e., the "regular" way), you can certainly bind off with 3. This method is a great way to both bind off and seam at the same time. It is very often used to seam the shoulders of a sweater. We'll be using it to bind off and seam the top of the Sweet Dreams Hat. Typically, the bind-off edge (i.e., the seam) is hidden on the inside, but I like the seam to be visible as a decorative element of this hat.

Step 1: Equally divide your sts and transfer them to 2 of your double-pointed needles (see Photo 1). You should have 10 (11, 12) sts on each needle, with the tail yarn on the right. The first and last sts of your round should now be aligned, each as the first st on the needles.

Step 2: With a third needle, knit the first st on both needles at the same time (see Photo 2). Do this by placing the right needle through the first st as if to knit, then place the right needle through the first st on the second needle as if to knit, then continue to knit both sts as a single st (see Photo 3). You'll have 1 st on your right needle as if you had knit only 1 regular st.

Step 3: Repeat step 2, then pull the first st on the right needle over the second st, just as you would for a standard bind-off (see Photo 4). Continue across the row until all sts are bound off.

How to Do a 3-Needle Bind-off

This technique is a great way to both bind off and seam at the same time. Typically, the bind-off edge (i.e., the seam) would be hidden on the inside, but for this hat our seam is visible as a decorative element.

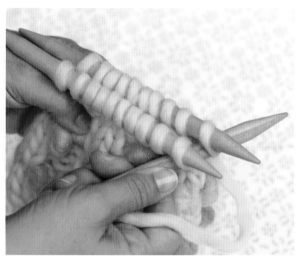

Photo 1: Equally divide stitches onto 2 double-pointed needles, keeping tail yarn on the right. Align first and last stitches of your round, each as the first stitch on your needles.

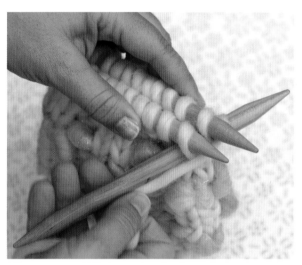

Photo 2: With a third needle, knit first stitch on both needles at same time. Place right needle through first stitch as if to knit, then place right needle through first stitch on second needle as if to knit, then knit both stitches as a single stitch.

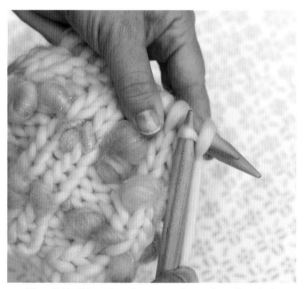

Photo 3: You'll have 1 stitch on your right needle as if you had knit only 1 regular stitch.

Photo 4: Repeat previous step, then pull first stitch on right needle over second stitch (as in a standard bind-off). Now continue across row until all stitches are bound off.

DASHING THROUGH THE SNOW HAT

Need a baby gift this afternoon? Let the Dashing through the Snow Hat save the day! I first made this hat for a photographer to use on her own new baby for their family Christmas card (hence the wintery name!), but I've also made it in many lighter-weight yarns for warmer weather babies, and the charm shines through whatever the season. It is deceptively simple to make — just knit a few rows of stockinette on size 19s with something bulky and then add a chunky accent yarn. Perfect for a new baby or for use as a parent-pleasing photography prop.

Skills Required: Knitting 2 stitches together, purling 2 stitches together, picking up stitches

Size: Fits newborns to 4 weeks/head size up to 14" (6–12 weeks/head size up to 15" or 3–6 months/head size up to 17"); finished piece measures approx 5½" (6½", 8") long by 6" (6½", 7") front to back

Gauge: 6 sts and 9 rows = 4"/10cm over St st

Notes: This hat is knit back and forth on straight or circular needles as a rectangle with some minimal, but important, shaping, then is folded over and sewn closed at the crown from front to back with the tail yarn. I prefer a knit-on cast-on for a more invisible seam, but you can use whatever method you prefer. The border I've shown is knit with 3 yarns, but you can use fewer if you like. The border is picked up with circulars, then the tassels are added. Be mindful of baby's curious fingers with the tassels.

Glossary of Abbreviations

approx	approximately	MC	main color
BO	bind off	p2tog/P2tog	purl 2 stitches together
CC-1, -2	contrasting colors (1, 2, etc.)	RS	right side
CO	cast on	st(s)	stitch(es)
dec	decrease/decreasing	St st	stockinette stitch
k2tog/K2tog	knit 2 stitches together	WS	wrong side

Materials

- 1 skein Cascade *Magnum* in #9478 Cotton Candy (123yd/112m - 8.8oz/250g; 100% wool) (MC)

- 1 skein Ozark Handspun *Opulent* in Secret Garden (50yd/46m - 3.5oz/100g; 65% mohair/35% wool) (CC-1)

- 1 hank Blue Sky Alpacas *Brushed Suri* in #907 Pink Lemonade (142yd/130m - 1.74oz/50g; 67% baby suri/22% merino wool/11% bamboo) (CC-2)

- US 19 (15mm) circular needles

- US 19 (15mm) straight needles (optional – you can knit the hat back and forth on circulars if you prefer)

- Yarn needle

- Tape measure

- Scissors

Knitting the Dashing through the Snow Hat

With US 19 (15mm) straights (or circulars) and MC, CO 18 (20, 22) sts, leaving a 15" tail for sewing crown together later.

FOR ALL SIZES:

Row 1: Knit.

Row 2: Purl.

Repeat Rows 1 and 2 until piece measures 3½" (4½", 5½") from CO edge, ending with a purl row. This will likely be after you have finished Row 6 (8, 10).

Begin dec sequence as follows on a knit row:

Row 1: Knit 8 (9, 10), k2tog, knit 8 (9, 10).

Row 2: Purl 7 (8, 9), p2tog, purl 8 (9, 10).

Row 3: For newborn size: Knit 3, k2tog, knit 2, k2tog, knit2, k2tog, knit 3. For 6–12 week size: knit 3, k2tog, knit 3, k2tog, knit 3, k2tog, knit 3. For 3–6 month size: Knit 3, k2tog, knit 4, k2tog, knit 4, k2 tog, knit 3.

Row 4: Purl 6 (7, 8), p2tog, purl 5 (6, 7).

BO purlwise (even though you will be on a knit row). If you are using the MC in your tassel, then cut tail yarn at the length of your tassel If you do not want the MC as part of the tassel, cut yarn and weave in end. Your finished piece so far should look like Photo 1 (shown in the 6–12 month size).

Sewing the Crown

To create the hat, thread the tail yarn of your CO edge through a yarn needle (or just use your fingers to weave the yarn back and forth to sew the seam). Fold the hat and with WS facing each other, sew sides together along the CO edge from front to back (see Photo 2). I like to sew it from the outside (i.e., the RS), rather than turn it inside out, so I can make sure that the seam is coming along as invisibly as possible.

Adding the Border

With US 19 (15.5mm) circulars, and CC-1 and CC-2 (and CC-3 for the turquoise hat), pick up 1 stitch in each row, plus 1 stitch at the midpoint, along the front edge of the hat with RS facing you (see Photo 3). You may choose to single, double, or even triple strand your choice of yarns to get the look you want.

BO and leave tails long enough to become part of tassel — about 5". If you prefer a wider border, purl back across the row, then BO as indicated.

Adding the Tassels

Determine your preferred length of your tassel — the length I've shown on the hats in the photos is about 5". Cut several pieces of CC-1 and CC-2 (and the MC, if you prefer) twice the tassel length (10").

Fold the tassel yarns in half, with your finger through the loop at the folded end. With the RS of the hat facing you, draw the folded end through the first stitch of the front edge of the hat (see Photo 4), and pull the loose ends through the folded loop. Pull the tassel to tighten the loop and trim ends as necessary.

Repeat with the same number of tassel yarns to match the other side.

Making the Dashing through the Snow Hat

Photo 1: This is the 6–12 month size fresh off the needles and ready for seaming the crown.

Photo 2: Sew up the crown with the tail yarn.

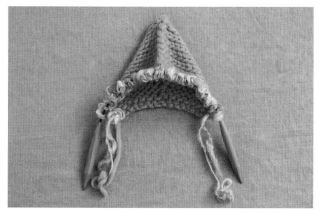

Photo 3: Pick up the stitches for the border around the face. Try to pick up 1 stitch in every row, plus 1 more at the midpoint.

Photo 4: Adding the tassel — this cute hat is almost done!

Variations

If you're looking for other ideas for this pattern, considering binding off with a coordinating color to give the bottom edge a little more definition. I've shown it in pink in the newborn size with my favorite texture-rich handspun as the border around the face, but I also love the chubbiness of a thick-n-thin like Malabrigo *Aquarella* mixed with the wispy Blue Sky Alpacas *Brushed Suri* and Cascade *Nikki* (as shown in the turquoise hat below). If you're looking for other yarn options, consider Blue Sky Alpacas *Bulky*, or double-strand a yummy worsted as the main color. Just be sure you check your gauge.

For the pink colorway shown on the baby at right, Cascade Magnum in cheerful Cotton Candy pink (MC at top) looks pretty edged with soft Brushed Suri in Pink Lemonade (CC-2 at bottom left) and the variegated hues of Opulent in Spring Garden (CC-1 at bottom right).

The bright blues, rich purples, and hint of lime make this a great combination for a boy or a girl.

For the turquoise colorway shown on the baby at left, use Cascade Magnum #9421 Blue Hawaii (MC on needle at top left), with three accent yarns — Cascade Nikki in #52132 Creekside (CC-1 at bottom left), Malabrigo Aquarella in #06 Minas (CC-2 at top right), and Blue Sky Alpacas Brushed Suri in #914 Agua (CC-3 at bottom right).

CHINNY CHIN CHINSTRAP CAP

If you're looking for something a bit more interesting to knit than a simple beanie, try this strapping little cap. It's a great gift idea because not only does it knit up surprisingly quickly, it is adorable on a baby of any age, so I've given a few options for larger sizes. And a chinstrap keeps a hat where it belongs, right on the baby's head, which means no more digging through the lost-and-found bin for your handknit treasure. There are two variations on the stocking tail, so pick the one that suits your fancy.

Skills Required: Knitting in the round on double-pointed needles, knitting 2 stitches together, slipping a stitch, slip knit pass decrease, picking up stitches, sewing a button, making an I-cord, making a pom-pom

Size: Fits newborn/head size up to 14" (3–6 months/head size up to 17"; 6–12 months/head size up to 19")

Gauge: Approx 8 sts and 10 rows = 4"/10cm over St st

Notes: This little hat is knit in the round from the cast-on edge around the forehead to the I-cord stocking tail. The earflaps are picked up and the chinstrap continues as an extension of one earflap. The pattern doesn't include a buttonhole, so choose a button that will easily fit through the stitches. The pattern includes two options for the stocking tail — one long and chunky with a large pom-pom, and one with a smaller pom-pom and a slimmer tail that is woven through the front of the hat.

Glossary of Abbreviations

approx	approximately	MC	main color	st(s)	stitch(es)
BO	bind off	rem	remaining	St st	stockinette stitch
CC	contrasting color	RS	right side	WS	wrong side
CO	cast on				
dec	decrease/decreasing				

k2tog/K2tog
knit 2 stitches together

skp/Skp
slip knit pass (also known as slip 1, knit 1, pass the slipped stitch over or sl1, k1, psso)

* repeat instructions following the asterisk as directed

Materials

- 1 skein Malabrigo *Gruesa* in #47 Green Spark (65yd/59m - 3.5oz/100g; 100% merino wool) (MC)
- A few yards Malabrigo *Gruesa* in #63 Natural (65yd/59m - 3.5oz/100g; 100% merino wool) (CC) for CO and pom-pom only
- US 17 (12.75mm) double-pointed needles
- US 13 (9mm) straight needles
- Stitch marker or scrap yarn
- Yarn needle
- Ruler or tape measure
- Small button
- Needle and thread
- Scissors

Photo 1: Move the final 6 stitches on the crown of the hat to a single double-pointed needle to prepare for the I-cord stocking tail.

Knitting the Chinny Chin Chinstrap Cap

With CC and US 17 (12.75mm) double-pointed needles, CO 22 (24, 26) sts and divide evenly over 4 needles, taking care not to twist sts.

Place marker and join to knit in the round. Knit the first st of this round with CC before cutting it to join MC.

Join MC and continue knitting in the round until piece measures 4½" (5", 5½") from the CO edge.

Begin dec sequence:

Round 1: *Knit 3 (4, 4), k2tog. Repeat from * to end of round. If you CO 22 or 26 sts, you will end with knit 2.

Round 2: Knit.

Round 3: *Knit 2 (3, 3), k2tog. Repeat from * to end of round. If you CO 22 or 26 sts, you will end with knit 2.

Round 4: Knit.

Round 5: *Knit1 (2, 2), k2tog. Repeat from * to end of round. If you CO 22 or 26 sts, you will end with knit 2.

Round 6: Knit.

Round 7: For newborn (3–6 month size), k2tog 4 (6) times, then knit the rest of the round (6 sts rem). Go on to choosing an I-cord. For 6–12 month size, *knit 1, k2tog, and repeat from * to end of round. You will end with knit 2.

Round 8: For 6–12 month size only, k2tog 4 times.

For all sizes, when you are down to 6 sts, place them all on 1 double-pointed needle to begin I-cord (see Photo 1) and follow instructions below for your preferred style of tail:

For Long and Chunky I-cord Tail

Rows 1–3: Knit.

Row 4: K2tog, knit 4 — you should now have 5 sts rem on your needle (see Photo 2).

Rows 5–7: Knit.

Row 8: K2tog, knit 3 — you should have 4 sts rem.

Rows 9–11: Knit.

Row 12: K2tog, knit 2 — you should have 3 sts rem.

Rows 13–15: Knit.

Row 16: K2tog, knit 1 — you should have 2 sts rem.

Rows 17–18: Knit.

Row 19: K2tog — you should have 1 last st rem.

Pull yarn through last st and knot, leaving a 6" tail for sewing pom-pom.

Make pom-pom (see page 17) and sew to end with the tail yarn.

For Slender I-cord Tail with Loop

Rows 1–2: Knit.

Row 3: K2tog, knit 4 — you should now have 5 sts rem on your needle.

Photo 2: Knit 2 stitches together (k2tog) for the I-cord stocking tail.

Mary Kate sports her Chinny Chin Chinstrap Cap, with the slender, looped version of the stocking tail, knit in the pretty purples of Malabrigo Aquarella in #15 Floresta (MC) with Gruesa in Natural (CC) for the border and pom-pom.

Rows 4–5: Knit.

Row 6: K2tog, knit 3 — you should have 4 sts rem.

Rows 7–8: Knit.

Row 9: K2tog, knit 2 — you should have 3 sts rem.

Rows 10–11: Knit.

Row 12: K2tog, knit 1 — you should have 2 sts rem.

Rows 13–14: Knit.

Row 15: K2tog — you should have 1 st rem.

Pull yarn through last st and knot, leaving a 6" tail for sewing pom-pom.

To loop your stocking tail, pull tail through a stitch on the front or side of the hat, depending on where you want your pom-pom to rest and which direction you want your loop to curl (see Photo 3, page 36). (I sometimes have a wonky-looking stitch smack on the front of my freshly knit item, making it easy to pick the spot to weave the tail.)

Make pom-pom (see page 17) and sew to end with the tail yarn.

Adding Earflaps and Chinstrap

Let's begin with the left earflap (as if you were wearing the hat), then we'll do the right side and chinstrap. I've chosen to use US 13s for the earflaps and chinstrap because a chinstrap knit on US 17s may be a bit cumbersome for going under a tiny chin. To locate your starting point for the left earflap, hold the hat with the RS facing you, CO edge at the top, and your round marker in front. Count over to the 8th (9th, 10th) sts to your right and using MC, pick up 5 sts by inserting the needle through the RS of the work, putting the new stitch on the needle, and drawing the needle through to the RS again. Follow the instructions for your size below.

FOR NEWBORN SIZE:

You should now have the WS facing you.

Row 1: Purl.

Row 2: SKP, knit 1, k2tog — you should have 3 sts rem on your needle. (This is one left-slanting dec,

Photo 3: To make the looped version of the stocking tail, pull the end of the tail through a stitch of your choice in the front of the cap. Be sure to do this before you add your pom-pom!

and one right-slanting dec, so you should have a nice tapered shape.)

Row 3: Purl.

BO and weave in end.

FOR 3–6 AND 6–12 MONTH SIZES:

You should now have the WS facing you.

Row 1: Purl.

Row 2: Knit.

Row 3: Purl.

Row 4: SKP, knit 1, k2tog — you should have 3 sts rem on your needle. (This is one left-slanting dec, and one right-slanting dec, so you should have a nice tapered shape.)

Row 5: Purl.

BO and weave in end.

For Right Earflap and Chinstrap

To locate your starting point for the right earflap (as if you were wearing the hat), hold the hat with the RS facing you, CO edge at the top, and your round marker in front. The earflap you just completed will be on your right, even though is it actually the left earflap for the hat.

Count over to the 4th (5th, 6th) sts to your left and using MC, pick up 5 sts by inserting the needle through the RS of the work, putting the new stitch on the needle, and drawing the needle through to the RS again. Your earflaps should be evenly spaced around the perimeter of the hat. Follow the instructions for your size above.

Follow instructions for the earflap for your size above, *but do not BO!* Continue in garter st (i.e., knit every row) until strap measures approx 6" (6¾", 7¼").

BO and weave in end.

Sew button securely to end of the outside of the chinstrap (see Photo 4).

Variations

If you don't have a bulky yarn handy, try double-stranding a favorite worsted to get your gauge. That opens up a whole new world of possibilities! You could also consider adding stripes of a novelty yarn.

Photo 4: Sew a button to the outside of the chinstrap near the bottom edge.

PARTY ON YOUR HEAD HAT

When I first saw *Cha-cha*, a ruffly ribbon yarn, I couldn't wait to start knitting up some happy baby hats! It adds the perfect amount of whimsy to any piece, and is especially fun to use as a chirpy trim on wee items. This lively little hat looks like a birthday cake to me — and you can't help but giggle just looking at it on a tiny noggin. It is truly like wearing a party on your head!

Skills Required: Knitting 2 stiches together, making a pom-pom

Size: Fits newborn/head size up to 14" (3–6 months/head size up to 17"; 6–12 months/head size up to 19")

Gauge: 12 sts and 12 rows = 4"/10cm over St st

Notes: This hat is knit flat, then is seamed up the back. You can work this general pattern in the round with just about any yarn, but because this particular ruffle yarn can be very tricky to knit with on double-pointed needles, I've written it as a flat pattern.

Glossary of Abbreviations

approx	approximately
CC-1,-2	contrasting colors (1, 2)
CO	cast on
dec	decrease/decreasing
k2tog	knit 2 stitches together
MC	main color
RS	right side
st(s)	stitch(es)
St st	stockinette stitch
WS	wrong side

* repeat instructions following the asterisk as directed

Materials

- 1 skein Malabrigo *Merino Worsted* in #27 Bobby Blue (210yd/192m – 3.5oz/100g; 100% merino wool) (MC)

- 1 skein Trendsetter Yarns *Cha-cha* in #31 Lime (65yd/59m – 3.5oz/100g; 47% wool/47% acrylic/6% nylon) (CC-1)

- 1 skein Colorful Nest *Purl Strand* in Moody Blues (150yd/137m - 4oz/117g; 99% merino/1% nylon) (CC-2)

- US 10 (6mm) straight needles

- Yarn needle

- Tape measure

- Scissors

Malabrigo's Merino Worsted in Natural (MC shown at lower left) is accented by two ribbon yarns by Trendsetter Yarns — silky, 100% nylon Segue in Blush (CC-2 shown at center), and ruffling Cha-cha in Rose (CC-1 shown at right).

The bright orange of Kitchen Sink Dyeworks Merino Silk Worsted in Poppi (MC shown at left) is complemented by the variegated reds and yellows of Colorful Nest Purl Strand in Red Sunset (CC-2 at center) and Trendsetter Yarns Cha-cha in zesty Lime (CC-1 at right).

Knitting the Party on Your Head Hat

This little hat is an easy knit — and when you see the ruffles begin to form, you'll probably start humming a cheery tune. The Trendsetter *Cha-cha* ribbon yarn, with its unique construction of open boxes along the top edge, will seem awkward to work with at first, but do not get discouraged — it's only yarn and you *can* master it. You'll find written instructions on the yarn band, and you can also view a terrific video of how to work with *Cha-cha* on Trendsetter's Web site at www.trendsetteryarns.com (which, incidentally, is how I learned).

Another note about *Cha-cha*: When you knit with it, the ruffles will form on the opposite side (the side facing away from you); when you purl with it, the ruffles will form on the side facing you. We want all of the ruffles to be on the outside (i.e., the RS) of our dazzling little hat, so we will be knitting with *Cha-cha* on the WS (odd-numbered) rows and purling with it on the RS (even-numbered) rows. Also, wherever *Cha-cha* is used in this pattern, it is worked for 2 rows (i.e., 1 knit row, then 1 purl row), then cut — not carried up the side of the work — so be sure you have your scissors handy to cut it and fold it over on itself to end a row, as directed in Trendsetter's written or video instructions.

With US 10 (6mm) needles and MC, CO 40 (44, 48) sts, leaving a 15" long tail for seaming the hat later. Carry the non-working yarn (except for *Cha-cha*, which will always be cut) up the side unless otherwise directed.

Row 1 (WS): *Purl 2, knit 2. Repeat from * across the row.

Row 2 (RS): *Knit 2, purl 2. Repeat from * across the row.

Row 3: Drop MC and with CC-1, knit. (see Photo 1.)

Row 4: With CC-1, purl. (see Photo 2.)

Row 5: Cut CC-1 and with MC, purl.

Row 6: With MC, knit.

Row 7: Drop MC and with CC-2, purl.

Row 8: With CC-2, purl.

Row 9: With CC-2, knit.

Row 10: With CC-2, knit.

Row 11: Drop CC-2 and with MC, purl.

Rows 12–14: With MC, knit.

Rows 15–16: With MC, purl.

Rows 17–18: With MC, knit.

Row 19: Drop MC and with CC-1, knit.

Photo 1: To begin knitting with Cha-cha, hold it at the back of the work. Insert point of right needle into first stitch on left needle (bright orange MC shown here), then pick up the top edge of the first open box of folded Cha-cha, from back to front of box, and pull through to knit the stitch.

Photo 2: After knitting a row with Cha-cha, you will purl the next row with Cha-cha. To purl, insert point of right needle purlwise into the existing Cha-cha stitch on the left needle, then pick up the top edge of the first open box, from back to front of box, and pull through to purl the stitch.

Row 20: With CC-1, purl.

Row 21: Cut CC-1 and with CC-2, purl.

Row 22: With CC-2, purl.

Row 23: Drop CC-2, and with MC, purl. For smallest newborn size, begin dec sequence now (see section below).

Rows 24–26: For 3–6 month and 6–12 month sizes: With MC, knit.

Row 27: Drop MC and with CC-2, purl. For 3–6 month size, begin dec sequence now.

Row 28: For 6–12 month size: With CC-2, purl.

Row 29: With CC-2, knit.

Row 30: With CC-2, knit.

Row 31: Drop CC-2 and with MC, purl. Begin dec sequence now.

Decreasing Sequence for All Sizes

Row 1: With MC, *knit 6, k2tog. Repeat from * across the row. For 3–6 month size only: knit 2, *knit 6, k2tog. Repeat from * across the row, ending with knit 2.

Row 2: With MC, knit.

Row 3: With MC, *knit 5, k2tog. Repeat from * across the row. For 3–6 month size only: knit 2, *knit 5, k2tog. Repeat from * across the row, ending with knit 2.

Row 4: With MC, knit.

Row 5: Cut MC and with CC-2, *knit 4, k2tog. Repeat from * across the row. For 3–6 month size only: knit 2, *knit 4, k2tog. Repeat from * across the row, ending with knit 2.

Row 6: With CC-2, knit.

Row 7: With CC-2, *knit 3, k2tog. Repeat from * across the row. For 3–6 month size only: knit 2, *knit 3, k2tog. Repeat from * across the row, ending with knit 2.

Row 8: With CC-2, purl.

Row 9: With CC-2, *knit 2, k2tog. Repeat from * across the row. For 3–6 month size only: knit 2, *knit 2, k2tog. Repeat from * across the row, ending with knit 2.

Row 10: With CC-2, purl.

YARN / AGE VARIATIONS
(newborn size materials on p. 39)

3–6 MONTH SIZE IN IVORY/PINK:

- 1 skein Malabrigo Merino *Worsted* in #63 Natural (210yd/192m - 3.5oz/100g; 100% merino wool) (MC)

- 1 hank Trendsetter Yarns *Cha-cha* in #28 Rose (65yd/59m - 3.5oz/100g; 47% wool/47% acrylic/6% nylon) (CC-1)

- 1 hank Trendsetter Yarns *Segue* in #300 Blush (120yd/110m - 3.5oz/100g; 100% nylon) (CC-2)

6–12 MONTH SIZE IN ORANGE/GREEN:

- 1 skein Kitchen Sink Dyeworks *Merino Silk Worsted* in Poppi (240yd/219m - 4oz/117g; 60% merino wool/40% silk) (MC)

- 1 hank Trendsetter Yarns *Cha-cha* in #31 Lime (65yd/59m - 3.5oz/100g; 47% wool/47% acrylic/6% nylon) (CC-1)

- 1 skein Colorful Nest *Purl Strand* in Red Sunset (150yd/137m - 4oz/117g; 99% merino wool/1% nylon) (CC-2)

Row 11: With CC-2, *knit 1, k2tog. Repeat from * across the row. For 3–6 month size only, knit 2: *knit 1, k2tog. Repeat from * across the row, ending with knit 2.

Finishing

For all sizes, draw yarn through remaining sts to close top of hat and knot. Sew up seam with CO tail yarn. Weave in all ends. Add a pom-pom if you like! (See page 17 for instructions.) I made the pom-poms shown on the blue/green and orange/green hats with equal amounts of MC and CC-2.

Variations

This pattern lends itself nicely to many worsted weight yarns as the MC. Treat yourself to any of the brilliant hues of silky worsteds from Alchemy Yarns of Transformation. If you're looking for a different accent yarn as CC-2, try *Trixie's Loopy Mohair* from Farmhouse Yarns. Can't get enough of the ruffles? Substitute a couple of rows of *Cha-cha* for the MC or CC-2 at the very top as a finishing touch!

CRISS-CROSS HAT

I love using stitches that look impressively complicated, but require very little effort on my part — like the one used in this zippy little hat. The big needles and chunky yarn really showcase the woven stitchwork, which is a simple 2-row pattern. You'll have your friends thinking you spent hours finely crafting each criss-cross, when actually you can knock this out in an afternoon!

Skills Required: Knitting 2 stitches together, purling 2 stitches together, slipping a stitch, passing a slipped stitch over, knitting into the back of a stitch

Size: Fits newborn/head size up to 14" (3–6 months/head size up to 17")

Gauge: 12 sts and 10 rows = 4"/10cm over pattern st

Notes: This hat is knit flat on US 19s, then is seamed up the back.

Glossary of Abbreviations

approx	approximately
BO	bind off
CC	contrasting color
CO	cast on
dec	decrease/decreasing
k2tog	knit 2 stitches together
MC	main color
p2tog/P2tog	purl 2 stitches together
psso	pass the slipped stitch over
RS	right side
sl/Sl	slip the stitch from the left needle to the right needle without working it
st(s)	stitch(es)
WS	wrong side
*	repeat instructions following the asterisk as directed

Materials

- 1 skein Aslan Trends *Del Sur* in #1 White (87yd/80m - 3.5oz/100g; 100% merino wool) (MC)

- 1 skein Malabrigo *Gruesa* in #184 Shocking Pink (for pink/white) or #48 Tuscan Sky (for blue/white) (65yd/59m - 3.5oz/100g; 100% merino wool) (CC)

- US 19 (15mm) straight needles

- Tape measure

- Yarn needle

- Scissors

For a baby girl, Del Sur in rich Nespresso (MC shown upper left) pairs sweetly with Cherry Bon Bon rayon ribbon from Judi & Co. (CC shown at bottom, and shown knit on page 49). For a boy, pair the Nespresso with the same rayon ribbon in the blues and browns of Dirty Denim (shown at right).

This lively Tuscan Sky blue and Shocking Pink Gruesa stand out nicely against the crisp white Del Sur.

Knitting the Criss-Cross Hat

This hat will fly off your 19s looking like you spent ages laboring over the stitches. For those who pooh-pooh the very idea of knitting a hat flat because they can't stand the notion of fussy seaming, let me tell you that a hat this small — knit on needles this big and with yarn this chunky — takes about 2 minutes to seam. Knit one and you'll see!

This woven stitch pattern is just 2 rows that are repeated until the hat is the appropriate size to begin the decreases.

With US 19 (15mm) straight needles and MC, CO 31 (37) sts. Cut MC.

Begin pattern st:

Row 1 (WS): With CC, *p2tog and leave sts on needle, then purl first st again and drop both sts from the needle. Repeat from * across the row, ending with knit 1.

Row 2 (RS): *Sl 1, knit 1, psso, but before dropping the slipped st from the left needle, knit into the back of it. Repeat from * across the row, ending with knit 1.

Repeat Rows 1 and 2 for 6 rows with CC. Cut CC, leaving 6" tail for seaming the CC band of the hat later. With MC, repeat Rows 1 and 2 until hat measures 4 ½" (5 ½") from CO edge, ending on a RS row.

Begin dec sequence as follows:

FOR NEWBORN SIZE:

Row 1: *P2tog and leave sts on needle, then purl first st again and drop both sts from the needle; p2tog. Repeat from * across row to last 3 sts, p2tog and leave sts on needle, then purl first st again and drop both sts from the needle, ending with knit 1.

Row 2: *Sl 1 knit 1, psso, knit 1*. Repeat from * across the row.

Row 3: P2tog across the row. You are ready for finishing!

FOR 3–6 MONTH SIZE:

Row 1: *P2tog and leave sts on needle, then purl first st again and drop both sts from the needle; p2tog. Repeat from * across the row, ending with knit 1.

Row 2: *Sl 1 knit 1, psso, knit 1*. Repeat from * across the row, ending with knit 1.

Row 3: *P2tog and leave sts on needle, then purl first st again and drop both sts from the needle; p2tog. Repeat from * across the row.

Row 4: *Sl 1 knit 1, psso, knit 1*. Repeat from * across the row.

Row 5: P2tog across the row.

Photo 1: A quick and easy way to make a floppy tassel topper for this hat — wrap your yarn 12 times (or more, if you prefer) around a piece of cardboard cut to the length you want your tassel. Tie at the top, cut at the bottom, and trim any ends as you see fit.

Finishing

Cut MC and thread through yarn needle. Draw through remaining sts and pull tightly to close the top of the hat. Use MC tail yarn to sew the MC portion of the hat and CC to seam the CC portion of the hat. Weave in all ends.

Add a floppy tassel if you like! Use a piece of cardboard cut in a 3" square and wrap the MC and CC yarns (held together) around the cardboard 12 times (see Photo 1). Slip an 8" piece of yarn under the wrapped yarn at the top edge of the cardboard and tie with a double knot. Carefully cut the wrapped yarn along the bottom edge of the cardboard and remove the cardboard. Trim ends if you like (I prefer mine a little wild) and attach to the top of the hat by threading the ends that are left at the top of the tassel through to the inside of the hat. Tie the end in a knot and weave into the inside of the hat.

Malabrigo Gruesa in scarlet Torero (CC shown at left) and chartreuse Lettuce (MC shown at right) make a merry combination for the 3-6 month size (shown on opposite page).

Variations

The stitchwork in this hat looks so pretty knit in bulky thick-n-thin handspuns like Malabrigo *Gruesa*, which I used here. Aslan Trends *Del Sur* and *Los Andes* are other great choices for this pattern. You should also consider treating yourself to a few skeins from a local spinner, or from any of the talented artisans at www.Etsy.com. Many will even custom dye the colorful skein of your dreams for you and the prices are very reasonable, considering the amount of work that goes into creating a skein of yarn. I would love to try it in a yarn from Springtree Road — her colorways are so rich and beautiful and the yarn is so soft, I can never pick just one. If you're thinking of whipping up this hat in other colors, keep in mind that the woven stitchwork will stand out best in lighter colors.

YARN / AGE VARIATIONS
(other newborn size materials on p. 39)

NEWBORN SIZE IN CHOCOLATE/ PINK RIBBON:

- 1 skein Aslan Trends *Del Sur* in #158 Nespresso (87yd/80m - 3.5oz/100g; 100% merino wool) (MC)

- 1 hank Judi & Co. ½" rayon ribbon in Cherry Bon Bon (100 yd/92m; 100% rayon) (CC)

3–6 MONTH SIZE IN RED/GREEN:

- 1 skein Malabrigo *Gruesa* in #37 Lettuce (65yd/59m - 3.5oz/100g; 100% merino wool) (MC)

- 1 skein Malabrigo *Gruesa* in #143 Torero (65yd/59m - 3.5oz/100g; 100% merino wool) (CC)

The chocolatey Del Sur in Nespresso (MC) looks delicious with hand-dyed Cherry Bon Bon ribbon (CC).

TWISTED TAFFY HAT

Keep those tiny noggins toasty with a twisty little hat! For this piece, I wanted to keep the design simple enough for beginners, but throw in an easy-to-learn stitch that turns an ordinary beanie into something much more interesting. The result is a beanie with a twist!

Skills Required: Knitting in the round on double-pointed needles, knitting 2 stitches together, making a pom-pom

Size: Fits newborn/head size up to 14" (3–6 months/head size up to 17")

Gauge: 7 ½ sts and 12 rows = 4"/10cm over St st

Notes: This hat is knit in the round on double-pointed needles. The diagonal spirals are created with right-twist stitches worked around the hat.

Glossary of Abbreviations

CC	contrasting color
CO	cast on
dec	decrease/decreasing
k2tog	knit 2 stitches together
MC	main color
RT	right twist (knit 2 sts together but do not drop sts from needle; knit first st, then drop both sts from left needle)
st(s)	stitch(es)
St st	stockinette stitch

* repeat instructions following the asterisk as directed

Materials

- 1 ball Lion Brand *Bolero* in #206 Lime Blue (55yd/50m – 3.5oz/100g; 100% wool) (MC)
- 1 skein Cascade *Magnum* in #9461 Lime Heather (123yd/112m - 8.8oz/250g; 100% wool) (CC).
- US 17 (12.75mm) double-pointed needles
- Stitch marker or scrap yarn
- Yarn needle
- Tape measure
- Scissors

The beautiful hues of thick-n-thin Bolero in Lime Blue at left, and Tutti Frutti at right, stand out nicely as a choice for the main color when paired with Magnum in Lime Heather (center).

Knitting the Twisted Taffy Hat

You'll begin by knitting a few rounds for the brim with the main color, then continue with a band of right twist stitchwork in a contrasting yarn, and work the crown of the hat in the main color to finish.

With MC and US 17 (12.75mm) double-pointed needles, CO 24 (28) sts. Place marker and join to knit in the round, taking care not to twist stitches.

Rounds 1–4: Knit. Cut MC (or carry up the inside for the next 5 rounds if you prefer).

Round 5: With CC, knit.

FOR NEWBORN SIZE:

Round 6: *Knit 4, RT. Repeat from * to end of round.

Round 7: *Knit 3, RT, knit 1. Repeat from * to end of round.

Round 8: *Knit 2, RT, knit 2. Repeat from * to end of round.

Round 9: *Knit 1, RT, knit 3. Repeat from * to end of round.

Round 10: *RT, knit 4. Repeat from * to end of round. Cut CC.

With MC, continue to knit until piece measures 4 1/4" from CO edge. Begin dec sequence:

Round 1: *Knit 4, k2tog. Repeat from * to end of round.

Round 2: *Knit 3, k2tog. Repeat from * to end of round.

Round 3: *Knit 2, k2tog. Repeat from * to end of round.

Round 4: *Knit 1, k2tog. Repeat from * to end of round. Proceed to Finishing.

FOR 3-6 MONTH SIZE:

Round 6: *Knit 5, RT. Repeat from * to end of round.

Round 7: *Knit 4, RT, knit 1. Repeat from * to end of round.

Round 9: *Knit 3, RT, knit 2. Repeat from * to end of round.

Round 10: *Knit 2, RT, knit 3. Repeat from * to end of round.

Blue Sky Alpacas Bulky in Blossom (CC) looks like strawberry mousse wrapped around the variegated pink/cream/caramel/sage green of Super Bulky Thick-n-Thin Merino in La Vie en Rose by Springtree Road (MC).

Round 11: *Knit 1, RT, knit 4. Repeat from * to end of round.

Round 12: *RT, knit 5. Repeat from * to end of round. Cut CC.

With MC, continue to knit until piece measures 4 3/4" from CO edge. Begin dec sequence:

Round 1: *Knit 5, k2tog. Repeat from * to end of round.

Round 2: *Knit 4, k2tog. Repeat from * to end of round.

Round 3: *Knit 3, k2tog. Repeat from * to end of round.

Round 4: *Knit 2, k2tog. Repeat from * to end of round.

Round 5: *Knit 1, k2tog. Repeat from * to end of round. Proceed to Finishing.

Finishing

Cut MC and thread through yarn needle. Draw through remaining sts and pull tightly to close the top of the hat. Weave in all ends. Add a pom-pom if you like, following the instructions on page 17.

Variations

I like the pairing of a variegated thick-n-thin yarn for the brim and crown, contrasted with a solid bulky to highlight the right twist stitchwork (like the hats shown here), but this pattern would be just as appealing knit in either of these as a single yarn. Need another idea? Add an I-cord stocking tail when you get to the crown — you'll have a cute new twist on an elf hat!

YARN VARIATIONS

NEWBORN SIZE WITH VARIEGATED PINK/TAN/:

- 1 skein Springtree Road *Super Bulky Thick-n-Thin Merino* in La Vie en Rose (130yd/118m - 4 oz/113g; 100% merino wool) (MC)

- 1 skein Blue Sky Alpacas *Bulky* in Blossom (45yd/41m - 3.5oz/100g; 50% alpaca/50% wool) (CC)

NEWBORN SIZE IN LIME WITH VARIEGATED PINKS/BLUES:

- 1 ball Lion Brand *Bolero* in #204 Tutti Frutti (55yd/50.3m - 3.5oz/100g; 100% wool) (MC)

- 1 skein Cascade *Magnum* in #9461 Lime Heather (123yd/112m - 8.8oz/250g; 100% wool) (CC)

CHUNKY BEANIE

Sometimes you just need a quick little beanie — nothing fancy, but certainly adorable. A simple beanie takes on an updated and sophisticated look when knit in chunky handspuns. Let these richly textured yarns do the work of looking like you spent hours knitting! These knit up so quickly, you can have a stack on hand as a last-minute gift for any occasion.

Skills Required: Knitting in the round on double-pointed needles, knitting 2 stitches together

Size: Fits newborn/head size up to 14" (3–6 months/head size up to 17"; 6–12 months/head size up to 19")

Gauge: 7 sts and 13 rows = 4"/10cm over St st

Notes: This is a straightforward knit in the round on double-pointed needles.

Glossary of Abbreviations

CC-1, -2	contrasting color (1,2)
CO	cast on
dec	decrease/decreasing
k2tog	knit 2 stitches together
MC	main color
st(s)	stitch(es)
St st	stockinette stitch

* repeat instructions following the asterisk as directed

Materials

- 1 skein Malabrigo *Aquarella* in #06 Minas (65yd/59m - 3.5oz/100g; 100% merino wool) (MC)

- 1 skein Colorful Nest *Purl Strand* in Fall Pansies (150yd/137m - 4oz/117g; 99% merino wool/1% nylon) (CC-1)

- 1 skein Malabrigo *Gruesa* in #37 Lettuce (65yd/59m - 3.5oz/100g; 100% merino wool) (CC-2)

- US 17 (12.75mm) double-pointed needles

- Stitch marker or scrap yarn

- Yarn needle

- Tape measure

- Scissors

The variegated violets, golds, and greens of Purl Strand *in Fall Pansies (CC-1 shown at bottom) lend themselves equally well to the deep purples in Aquarella Minas (MC, shown in center) and the chartreuse tones in Aquarella Lettuce (CC-2 shown at top).*

Perfect for autumn (from bottom to top) — Aquarella in deep Indigo (MC), Purl Strand in multi-toned Late Summer (CC-1), and Aquarella in Golden Sunset (CC-2).

Watermelon tones make up this juicy combination for the 6–12 month size — Purl Strand in pretty pinks and greens of Spring Garden (CC-1, ball in center) and Aquarella in girlish Shocking Pink (CC-2, far right). Not shown in this photo is chartreuse Aquarella in Lettuce (MC), which is the same yarn used as CC-2 for the newborn size.

Knitting the Chunky Beanie

This little beanie is worked in the round from the brim to the crown. You'll begin with a garter stitch border in the main color (shown in purple Minas in the newborn size, Indigo in the 3–6 month, and green Lettuce in the 6–12 month), then work in stockinette stitch (i.e., knit all rounds) for the remainder of the hat.

With MC and US 17 (12.75mm) double-pointed needles, CO 22 (24, 28) sts. Place marker and join to knit in the round, taking care not to twist stitches.

Round 1: Knit.

Round 2: Purl.

Round 3: Knit.

Round 4: Purl.

Round 5: Knit.

With MC and CC-1 held together, knit 4 (5, 5) more rounds. Cut MC.

With CC-1 and CC-2 held together, knit 4 (5, 5) more rounds. Cut CC-1.

Continue knitting in the round with CC-2 until piece measures 4¼" (4¾", 5½") from CO edge.(Just a note — if you are knitting close to gauge, this will probably be now.)

Begin dec sequence:

Round 1: *Knit 3 (4, 5), k2tog. Repeat from * to end of round, ending with knit 2 for newborn size.

Round 2: Knit.

YARN / AGE VARIATIONS
(newborn size materials on p. 55)

3–6 MONTH SIZE IN DARK BLUE/ORANGE:

- 1 skein Malabrigo *Aquarella* in #88 Indigo (65yd/59m - 3.5oz/100g; 100% merino wool) (MC)

- 1 skein Colorful Nest *Purl Strand* in Late Summer (150yd/137m - 4oz/117g; 99% merino wool/1% nylon) (CC-1)

- 1 skein Malabrigo *Gruesa* in #96 Sunset (65yd/59m - 3.5oz/100g; 100% merino wool) (CC-2)

6–12 MONTH SIZE IN GREEN/HOT PINK:

- 1 skein Malabrigo *Aquarella* in #37 Lettuce (65yd/59m - 3.5oz/100g; 100% merino wool) (MC)

- 1 skein Colorful Nest *Purl Strand* in Spring Garden (150yd/137m - 4oz/117g; 99% merino wool/1% nylon) (CC-1)

- 1 skein Malabrigo *Gruesa* in #184 Shocking Pink (65yd/59m - 3.5oz/100g; 100% merino wool) (CC-2)

Round 3: *Knit 2 (3, 4), k2tog. Repeat from * to end of round, ending with knit 2 for newborn size.

Round 4: Knit.

Round 5: *Knit 1 (2, 3), k2tog. Repeat from * to end of round, ending with knit 2 for newborn size.

For newborn and 3–6 month size, you are ready for finishing!

For 6–12 month size:

Round 6: Knit.

Round 7: *Knit 2, k2tog. Repeat from * to end of round.

Finishing

Cut CC-2 and thread through yarn needle. Draw through remaining sts and pull tightly to close the top of the hat. Weave in all ends.

Variations

I hope you will use this very basic pattern as a starting point for your own chunky hat designs — play with the color striping, or consider adding earflaps. If you're not quite ready to modify a pattern, you can add a tassel, yarn bow, or an oversized pompom — any of those would look fun perched on top!

WRAPS & BLANKETS

So cozy and warm!

Birthday Wrap

Hexagonal Hoodie

Lucky Seven Pinwheel Blanket

Big Zig Blanket

Later Gator Blanket

Starry Night Blanket

BIRTHDAY WRAP

You can't deny that there's something decidedly celebratory about this light and airy little blanket. The brilliant contrast of the lime green wispy soft mohair against the festive ribbons in the hot pink loopy mohair is as stunningly pretty as it is unexpected, a joyous combination meant for a special occasion like heralding a birth. The vivid colors, countless tiny bows, and cheery ruffle seem to sing "Happy Birthday" right from your needles. In fact, I designed the one in the photo for my own daughter.

Skills Required: Knitting into the front and back of a stitch, picking up stitches

Size: Approx 26" x 40" and very stretchy

Gauge: Approx 8 sts and 10 rows = 4"/10cm over St st

Notes: The decorative *Ribbon Ball* yarn, with its hand-tied satin ribbons and sparkly thread, is not meant for daily use and babies should not be left unattended with it. However, the basic pattern lends itself well to more practical yarn substitutions, and the blanket can easily be enlarged by simply adding rows of the main color in multiples of 10 or by adding more stitches. The Birthday Wrap is knit in easy garter stitch; to add the ruffle, stitches are picked up along all four edges and knit back and forth on circular needles.

Glossary of Abbreviations

approx	approximately
BO	bind off
CC	contrasting color
CO	cast on
kfb/Kfb	knit into the front and back of a single stitch, increasing by 1 stitch
MC	main color
RS	right side
st(s)	stitch(es)
St st	stockinette stitch

Materials

- 1 ball Katia *Ingenua* in #29 Green (153yd/140m - 1.76oz/50g; 78% mohair/ 13% nylon/9% wool) (MC)

- 4 balls Be Sweet *Ribbon Ball* in Bouquet (95yd/87m - 1.76oz/50g; mohair with hand-tied ribbon) (CC)

- US 19 (15mm) 24" (or longer) circular needles

- US 19 (15mm) straight needles (optional; you can knit the blanket back and forth on circulars if you prefer)

- Yarn needle

- Scissors

A lovely pair — flirtatious Ribbon Ball in Bouquet from Be Sweet (CC at left) and Ingenua in #29 Green from Katia (MC).

A soothing duo — Trixie's Loopy Mohair in Harvest from Farmhouse Yarns (CC at left) and silky Brushed Suri in Whipped Cream from Blue Sky Alpacas (MC).

About *Ribbon Ball:* I double-stranded it through-out this piece, including the ruffle, and after going through three balls of it, lacked about 10 stitches to complete the ruffle. Aghhh! If you prefer to get away with purchasing three balls, rather than four, you could easily bind off using a single strand of *Ribbon Ball* and still have a luxurious ruffle. For that matter, you could knit up a swatch of the ruffle in a single strand and see if you like it. I would, however, suggest that you still double-strand the stripes in the blanket. You really lose the va-va-voom of the *Ribbon Ball* with just two single-stranded rows.

Knitting the Birthday Wrap

With MC and US 19 (15mm) straights (or circulars, if you prefer), CO 40 sts. You will carry the MC yarn up the side throughout when you alternate with the CC.

Knit 10 rows with MC, carrying yarn up the side.

Knit 2 rows of CC, cut yarn, and knot.

Knit 10 rows of MC, carrying yarn up the side.

Knit 2 rows of CC, cut yarn, and knot.

Knit 10 rows of MC, carrying yarn up the side.

Knit 2 rows of CC, cut yarn, and knot.

Knit 10 rows of MC.

BO very loosely and weave in all ends.

Adding the Ruffle

To add the ruffle, you'll be picking up stitches and knitting along all 4 sides as if they were one tortur-ously long row, then stitching up the corner. You'll need your circulars to hold this many stitches. Fear not — although it is a lot of stitches, it's just for a couple of rows and the result is so worth the effort!

With double-stranded CC and circular needles, pick up a total of 172 sts (i.e., ideally, 1 stitch in every row on both sides and 1 stitch in every stitch along the top and bottom, 40+40+46+46), or as close to that as you can. If you're a tight knitter, you may have a bit of trouble wrestling your 19s through those stitches. Don't fret. Just pick up as many as you can, because who's going to know?

Photo 1: After binding off the ruffle, you will have a gap at one corner that needs to be sewn.

Photo 2: To finish, use the tail yarn and a yarn needle to sew the edges together where they meet in the corner.

Photo 3: Weave in the ends and you're finished with your beautiful Birthday Wrap — a cause for celebration indeed!

It will still be beautiful, but the more stitches you can pick up and the more evenly they are distributed, the more you will preserve the elasticity of the blanket.

Row 1: Knit.

Row 2: Purl.

Row 3: Kfb all sts (344 sts).

BO very loosely, leaving a tail yarn for sewing. Sew the gap in the corner of the ruffle (see photos). Knot and weave in ends.

Variations

If you like the idea of contrasting a wispy yarn with a chunky counterpart, consider mixing an angora, brushed suri, or another mohair with something like a bulky thick-n-thin merino. For my next version, I think I'll take the more practical route and try either Blue Sky Alpacas *Brushed Suri* or Be Sweet *Brushed Mohair* as the main yarn. They're both deliciously soft. I'd bet either of them would be stunning with Farmhouse Yarns *Trixie's Loopy Mohair*, a double strand of Trendsetter *Joy*, or another fun novelty yarn.

HEXAGONAL HOODIE

I love the idea of a hooded blanket for a baby gift. But it has always bothered me that a typical diamond/square blanket with the hood in the corner doesn't leave much blanket to cover the baby — you're left with the skimpy points of the diamond to do much of the covering that a blanket should do. So I came up with this hexagonal version. The optional hood is easily removable if you want to take it off later. Not only is the pattern a breeze to memorize (barely three rows), but with 17s and chunky yarns you can whip it up in a few hours. Here's an idea — make it a "grow with me" blanket and add a row or two every year on the baby's birthday. Just pick up stitches around the perimeter and start knitting. He'll have a rug to take to college!

Skills Required: Knitting in the round on double-pointed and circular needles, knitting into the front and back of a stitch, slip knit pass decrease, making a pom-pom

Size: Newborn/car seat size measures approx 24" in diameter; larger size approx 34" in diameter

Gauge: Approx 8 sts and 10 rows = 4"/10cm over St st

Notes: This nifty little blanket is knit from the inside to the outer edges. You begin on double-pointed needles, then transfer to circulars. The optional hood is a simple stockinette stitch triangle that is sewn on with the tail yarn and can be easily removed.

Glossary of Abbreviations

approx	approximately	MC	main color
BO	bind off	RS	right side
CC	contrasting color	skp/Skp	slip knit pass (also known as slip1, knit1, pass the slipped stitch over or sl1, k1, psso)
CO	cast on		
k2tog/K2tog	knit 2 stitches together	st(s)	stitch(es)
kfb/Kfb	knit into the front and back of a single stitch, increasing by 1 stitch	St st	stockinette stitch
		WS	wrong side

Materials

- 2 skeins Colorful Nest *Purl Strand* in Late Summer (150yd/137m - 4oz/117g; 99% merino wool/1% nylon) (MC)

- 2 skeins Aslan Trends *Del Sur* in #9 Sour Apple (87yd/80m - 3.5oz/100g; 100% merino wool) (CC)

- US 17 (12.75mm) circular needles

- US 17 (12.75mm) set of double-pointed needles, but US 15s (10mm) or even US 13s (9mm) will do

- Scrap yarn to use as stitch markers (two colors)

- Yarn needle

- Tape measure

- Scissors

The tart Sour Apple Del Sur from Aslan Trends (CC shown at center) perfectly complements the multi-toned blue hues of Late Summer (MC at top, as shown in blanket on opposite page) and the cheery pinks of Spring Garden (MC at bottom, as shown in blanket on page 68) — both Purl Strand by Colorful Nest.

Knitting the Hexagonal Hoodie

This is really one of my favorite patterns, but I must warn you of the frustration you may (OK — most undoubtedly will) suffer as you try to cast on and then knit the first 6 stitches in the round on the size 17 double-pointeds. I know — it is hard enough to get started with so few stitches on normal-size needles, much less the broomsticks I'm asking you to use here. But once you tame that unruly first round of stitches, you'll be amazed at how submissive they become. And don't fret if you can't track down a set of 17s — you can use 15s or even 13s to get started. You'll just be using them for the first few rounds in the center of the blanket and the difference in needle sizes for a few rounds is not going to detract from the charm of this blanket one bit.

For the increase rounds beyond Round 2, you'll be adding 12 new stitches — 2 into each of the 6 segments of the hexagon. So, if you're still with me, let's begin:

With US 17 (12.75mm) double-pointed needles and MC, CO 6 sts — 2 on each needle. Place marker and join to knit in the round, taking care not to twist sts (see Photo 1).

Photo 1: With 2 stitches on each needle, place marker (such as the scrap of purple yarn on the left) and join to knit in the round.

Round 1: Knit.

Round 2: Kfb of each st. (You should now have 12 sts — 4 on each needle. I'll count them for you for the first few rounds, then you're on your own, but just know that you should always have a number that is divisible by 6.)

Round 3: Knit.

Round 4: Kfb of the 1st of each needle, kfb of the middle 2 sts of each needle, kfb of the last st on each needle. Knit all other sts. (Note that for Round 4 only you'll actually kfb of all 4 sts on each needle. You should now have 24 sts — 8 on each needle.)

Rounds 5 and 6: Knit.

Rounds 4, 5, 6 are repeated for the entire rest of the blanket — that's it! When you have too many sts to fit on double-pointeds, or too many to conveniently count to the middle 2 sts (about Round 13 or so), transfer them to circulars. IMPORTANT NOTE: As you transfer your sts to your circulars, place markers to divide the sts into 6 even sections, using a contrasting marker as your round marker. For the remainder of the project, you no longer have to count to the middle 2 sts, because your markers should now be between those middle 2 sts. You should have a total of 6 markers showing 6 equal segments.

To be clear, after you have transferred to circulars, your 3-round pattern for the remainder of this blanket is this:

• Kfb of the st before and after each marker. Knit all other sts.

• Knit.

• Knit.

Continue these 3 rounds until you have completed a total of 24 rounds.

FOR NEWBORN/CAR SEAT BLANKET:

Cut MC and continue pattern with CC for 16 more rounds, or until your desired size. NOTE: This is a stockinette stitch blanket, meaning the edges will curl inward a bit (see photo on page 68). If that isn't your preference, then consider alternating a knit round with a purl round for the last 4 rounds.

BO loosely purlwise and weave in ends. If you want to add the hood, leave the tail yarn to use for sewing.

The larger size of the Hexagonal Hoodie is just right for 14-month-old Jeannie.

FOR LARGER BLANKET:

Continue pattern with MC for 10 more rounds.

Cut MC and continue pattern for 7 rounds with CC.

Drop but do not cut CC, and with MC continue pattern for 2 rounds.

Cut MC, and with CC, continue pattern for 4 rounds, or until your desired size. NOTE: This is a stockinette stitch blanket, meaning the edges will curl inward a bit. See instructions for newborn size (above) for an alternative.

BO loosely purlwise and weave in ends. If you want to add the hood, leave the tail yarn to use for sewing.

Knitting the Optional Hood

The hood is a simple stockinette stitch triangle. It is important that you know how to do two different decreases to create a nice even triangle — the k2tog (knit 2 together), which creates a right-slanting decrease, and one of its mirror buddies, the skp (slip 1, knit 1, pass the slipped stitch over), which creates a left-slanting decrease. There are many other ways to increase and decrease, so feel free to substitute your favorite technique, but these are two of the

Photo 2: Match the point of your hood with one point of the blanket, with wrong sides facing each other. Now you can sew them together with the tail yarns.

ones I use most frequently. (Please see the quick tutorial and discussion of the wonders of the k2tog and skp decreases on page 102 in the Tab Top Cocoon pattern.)

With US 17 (12.75mm) circulars and CC, CO 18 (26) sts. Work in St st, decreasing as follows:

Every RS (knit) row: Knit 1, skp, knit to 3 st from end, k2tog, knit 1.

The cheery pinks of Colorful Nest Purl Strand in Spring Garden (MC) complement the Sour Apple Del Sur by Aslan Trends (CC).

Every WS row: Purl.

When you have 6 sts remaining, work the WS (purl) row as usual. Then continue as follows:

RS row: Knit 1, skp, k2tog, knit 1.

WS row: Purl.

RS row: Skp, k2tog.

BO and leave tail yarn to use for sewing hood to blanket.

Sewing Hood to Blanket

Lay your blanket out flat, with the WS facing up. Match the point of your hood with one point of the blanket, with WS of the hood and blanket facing each other (see Photo 2). Use the tail yarns from the hood and blanket to sew in place. Add a pom-pom (see page 17 for instructions) if you like!

Variations

The Hexagonal Hoodie is such a fun and quickly rewarding pattern that I invite you to try it in every yarn you can get your hands on. The blanket is knit from the center outward, so you can make this any size you like. It works great on a bulky scale with yarns of different textures such as what I've shown here, but you will get a totally different look with a bulky yarn in a different fiber blend like Blue Sky Alpacas *Outer* (an organic cotton/superwash wool blend). Go down a couple of needle sizes and use a few different flavors of delicious worsted like Tahki *Tinka* or Kitchen Sink Dyeworks *Merino Silk Worsted*. Keep in mind, however, that the optional hood pattern is written to fit a baby's head at the gauge specified.

LUCKY SEVEN PINWHEEL BLANKET

Round blankets are so satisfying to knit for many reasons. They are invariably looked upon by non-knitters as a true feat of knitting expertise — as if no one could possibly knit a circle unless they were really one of the knitting elite. Second, the pattern is so ridiculously easy to memorize — and equally easy to figure out where you are if you set it down and don't get back to it for months — that it is actually a great adventuresome beginner's project. Third, once you get the hang of it, you can easily add all sorts of interesting stitches and lacework or, since you are knitting from the inside toward the outer edge, you can knit ad infinitum — don't stop on my account where this pattern says you must. Incidentally, I designed this blanket with seven spirals because I have no hope of ever having the time to knit each of my seven children their own blanket. The idea of seven happy spirals dancing around in a single blanket will have to do.

Skills Required: Knitting on double-pointed needles, knitting in the round on circular needles, making a yarn over

Size: Approx 26" in diameter

Gauge: 8 sts and 8 rows = 4"/10cm over St st

Notes: This round blanket is knit from the inside to the outer edges. You begin on double-pointed needles, then transfer to circulars. Here's a trick — if you prefer your spirals to swirl to the left, rather than to the right as they will in this pattern, simply begin each segment with your knit stitches, rather than with your yarn over.

Glossary of Abbreviations

approx	approximately
BO	bind off
CC-1, -2	contrasting colors (1, 2)
CO	cast on
MC	main color
st(s)	stitch(es)
St st	stockinette stitch
yo/Yo	yarn over

* repeat instructions following the asterisk as directed

Materials

- 3 hanks Blue Sky Alpacas *Bulky* in #1210 Blossom (45yd/41m - 3.5oz/100g; 50% alpaca/50% wool) (MC)

- 1 skein Farmhouse Yarns *Trixie's Loopy Mohair* in Chocolate Covered Cherries (100yd/91m - 3.5oz/100g; 90% kid mohair/10% nylon) (CC-1)

- 1 hank Blue Sky Alpacas *Brushed Suri* in #907 Pink Lemonade (142yd/130m - 1.76oz/50g; 67% baby suri/22% merino wool/11% bamboo) (CC-2)

- US 19 (15mm) circular needles

- US 17 (12.75mm) set of double-pointed needles, but US 15s (10mm) or even US 13s (9mm) will do for the first few rounds

- Scrap yarn to use as round markers (two colors)

- Yarn needle

- Tape measure

- Scissors

Bulky in Blossom pink (MC shown at left) is paired with flirty Trixie's Loopy Mohair in Chocolate Covered Cherries (CC-1 at center) and wispy Brushed Suri in Pink Lemonade (CC-2 at right).

As an alternate combination, consider (from left to right): Cascade Magnum in #9421 Blue Hawaii (100% wool) for MC with Aslan Trends Litoral in #1315 Ocean (50% acrylic/50% polyamide) and Blue Sky Alpacas Brushed Suri in #904 Fudgesicle as CC-1 and CC-2.

Photo 1: With your double-pointed needles, cast on 7 stitches and place a marker (a little piece of scrap yarn works well). Be careful not to twist the stitches.

Knitting the Lucky Seven Pinwheel Blanket

This happy little blanket is delightfully simple to knit and just might become one of your "go-to" patterns when the time rolls around for that next baby gift. That being said, if you've already tried (or at least read) the pattern for the Hexagonal Hoodie Blanket on page 66, then you'll be well acquainted with the one downside to this pattern — it's the bit about casting on so few stitches on such huge double-pointed needles (in this case, 7 stitches on US 17s — oh, I can hear you screaming from here). Please take a moment to read that pattern now, if you need some encouragement. Be heartened by the fact that if you prefer to use smaller, more manageable, or more easy-to-find double-pointeds to get started (US 15s or 13s), then feel free. It's the least I can offer you. Just don't forget to switch over to the largest double-pointeds you have once you get going, then to the US 19 circulars when you have too many stitches to handle on your double-pointeds. Trust me that you will be richly rewarded in the end by the penance you serve knitting these first few wicked rounds.

So let's begin:

With US 17 (12.75mm) double-pointed needles and MC, CO 7 sts, as shown in Photo 1. Place marker (I use a little piece of scrap yarn tied around my needle), taking care not to twist sts. Knit 1 round. Continue in pattern st as follows:

Round 1: *Yo, knit 1, place marker. Repeat from * to end of round. You should have 7 markers on your needles. Remember to use a contrasting color for your round marker. You'll be sliding the marker, then doing your yo for each of the 7 segments.

Round 2 and all even-numbered rounds: Knit.

Round 3: *Yo, knit 2. Repeat from * to end of round.

Round 5: *Yo, knit 3. Repeat from * to end of round.

Round 7: *Yo, knit 4. Repeat from * to end of round. Transfer to US 19 circulars if you are running out of room on your double-pointed needles.

Round 9: *Yo, knit 5. Repeat from * to end of round.

Continue the pattern st in this manner, alternating even-numbered rounds of plain knitting with odd-numbered rounds of knitting one additional stitch in each segment.

Do not fear if your blanket starts to looks like a large jellyfish blob or enormous jaunty beret after a few rounds (as mine does in Photo 2). Embrace the clunkiness and knit on. That's part of the mystique.

To add the stripe as shown, work until you have completed the round of plain knitting after

Photo 2: You may not be able to resist the urge to try this on — the thought of using this pattern to knit yourself a beret sometime down the road is so tantalizing.

the "*Yo, knit 8." Then continue as follows:

Drop, but do not cut, MC. With 2 strands of CC-1 and 1 strand of CC-2: *Yo, knit 9. Repeat from * to end of round.

Knit 1 round.

Cut and knot CC-1 and CC-2, and with MC continue in the pattern st, ending with "*Yo, knit 14. Repeat from * to end of round."

BO loosely and weave in ends.

For a larger blanket, simply continue the pattern until you have your desired size.

Variations

If you like the idea of this blanket, but don't care for the holes created by the yarn overs, you can substitute a different increase technique such as knitting into the front and back of a stitch (kfb) for every yarn over (yo) in the pattern. If you'd like to give it a try, follow these slight modifications to the first few rounds:

Round 1: Knit.

Round 2: Kfb of all sts.

Round 3: *Kfb, knit 1. Repeat from * to end of round.

Round 4: Knit.

Round 5: *Kfb, knit 2. Repeat from * to end of round.

Continue in this manner, alternating even-numbered rounds of plain knitting with odd-numbered rounds of knitting 1 additional stitch in each segment.

This pattern will also lend itself nicely to just about any yarn type or needle size, depending on your preference. I say that because if you have the patience to knit with laceweight on US 4s, you can carelessly cast the notion of my gauge into the wind and set off on this exact pattern and end up with a lovely blanket. Unlike some fiendish patterns that would have you begin at the outside edge and knit inward, you alone control the destiny of the finished product since you are starting at the center and knitting for as long as your yarn (or patience) will last.

BIG ZIG BLANKET

If you have a baby or toddler in your life, you already know that you can't have enough thick and comfy blankets on hand. They're soft enough for snuggling a snoozing newborn and can then do double duty as a cushy floor mat for a curious babe. This one is knit in a bulky organic cotton/superwash wool blend, making it especially soft and lofty (and machine-washable!) — a perfect gift for a new mother. The bold, geometric patterns of these ziggity-zaggaty panels will keep you interested while you knit and will add a modern flair to any nursery.

Skills Required: Knitting into the front and back of a stitch, knitting through the back loop, knitting 2 stitches together, picking up stitches, sewing a mattress stitch

Size: Approx 24" x 34"

Gauge: 8 sts and 10 rows = 4"/10cm over St st

Notes: This blanket is knit in 3 separate panels, which are then sewn together. The border is picked up after the panels are joined.

Glossary of Abbreviations

approx	approximately
BO	bind off
CC	contrasting color
CO	cast on
kfb/Kfb	knit into the front and back of a single stitch, increasing by 1 stitch
LT	left twist (skip first st and knit second st through back loop; knit both sts together through back loop, then drop both sts from left needle)
MC	main color
RS	right side
RT	right twist (knit 2 sts together but do not drop sts from needle; knit first st, then drop both sts from left needle)
st(s)	stitch(es)
St st	stockinette stitch
WS	wrong side

Materials

- 4 hanks Spud & Chloë *Outer* in #7211 Rocket (60yd/55m - 3.4oz/100g; 65% superwash wool/35% organic cotton) (MC)
- 3 hanks Spud & Chloë *Outer* in #7208 Cornsilk (60yd/55m - 3.4 oz/100g; 65% superwash wool/35% organic cotton) (CC)
- US 17 (12.75mm) 29" (or longer) circular needles
- US 17 (12.75mm) straight needles (optional — you can use the circulars to knit the panels back and forth if you prefer)
- Yarn needle
- Scissors
- Iron (for optional steam-blocking)
- Rust-free pins (for optional steam- or spritz-blocking)

Machine-washable, wool/cotton blend Outer by Spud & Chloë shown in happy pinky-red Rocket (MC at center) with warm, buttery Cornsilk (CC).

Spud & Chloë Outer in a muted palette of Sandbox (MC) wrapped around soothing blue Bayou (CC at center).

Knitting the Big Zig Blanket

You'll be knitting 3 individual panels for this blanket. Don't be daunted by the stitchwork, because it isn't nearly as complex as it may look. Panels 1 and 3 (worked in MC) are knit using the same pattern — the mirror image is achieved by beginning Panel 3 a few rows later in the pattern. The left twist and right twist stitches used in Panels 1 and 3 are only slightly tricky for the first few stitches, but they will come along much easier after you have a row under your belt. If you can knit 2 stitches together and knit through the back loop, you can swing this. Panel 2 is strictly knit and purl stitches — what could be simpler than that?

All that being said, if you like the idea of this blanket but don't think you want to tackle sewing 3 separate panels together, I've written the patterns for each panel so that they can be adapted easily to being knit consecutively as one continuous piece. Simply cast on enough stitches for all 3 panels (i.e., 24 stitches x 3 panels = 72 stitches) and begin reading the first row of all 3 panels, then the second row, etc. Depending on your mood (or your skill level), you can knit the entire blanket as a no-sew, single piece in one color, or if you're undaunted by multiple balls of yarn hanging from your work, you can knit it in multiple colors using a circular needle to hold all of the stitches.

I've added a 3-stitch stockinette edging at both ends of the rows to provide a visual buffer between the changing patterns in the panels. In other words, the first 3 and last 3 stitches of each row are the stockinette border and are not part of the zigzag pattern repeat. Should you want to make any of these panels wider by adding another horizontal repeat of the pattern, remember to take this into account.

Panel 1 (knit with MC)

With US 17 (12.75mm) straights (or circulars, if you prefer) and MC, CO 24 sts.

Row 1: Knit 3, LT 3 times, knit 3, LT 3 times, knit 6.

Row 2 and all WS rows (ending with Row 16): Purl.

Row 3: Knit 4, LT 3 times, knit 3, LT 3 times, knit 5.

Row 5: Knit 5, LT 3 times, knit 3, LT 3 times, knit 4.

Row 7: Knit 6, LT 3 times, knit 3, LT 3 times, knit 3.

Row 9: Knit 6, RT 3 times, knit 3, RT 3 times, knit 3.

Row 11: Knit 5, RT 3 times, knit 3, RT 3 times, knit 4.

Row 13: Knit 4, RT 3 times, knit 3, RT 3 times, knit 5.

Row 15: Knit 3, RT 3 times, knit 3, RT 3 times, knit 6.

Repeat Rows 1–16 two more times, then repeat Rows 1–6. This will give you a total of 54 rows (i.e., 16 + 16 + 16 + 6 = 54). (See Photo 1.)

BO loosely and weave in ends.

Panel 2 (knit with CC)

With US 17 (12.75mm) straights (or circulars, if you prefer) and CC, CO 24 sts.

Row 1: Knit 3, purl 1, knit 16, purl 1, knit 3.

Row 2: Purl 3, knit 2, purl 14, knit 2, purl 3.

Photo 1: You'll use left twist and right twist stitches to make the zigzagging panels 1 and 3 (see Photo next page).

Row 3: Knit 3, purl 3, knit 12, purl 3, knit 3.

Row 4: Purl 3, knit 4, purl 10, knit 4, purl 3.

Row 5: Knit 3, purl 5, knit 8, purl 5, knit 3.

Row 6: Purl 3, knit 6, purl 6, knit 6, purl 3.

Row 7: Knit 3, purl 7, knit 4, purl 7, knit 3.

Row 8: Purl 3, knit 8, purl 2, knit 8, purl 3.

Row 9: Knit 3, purl 18, knit 3.

Row 10: Purl 4, knit 16, purl 4.

Row 11: Knit 5, purl 14, knit 5.

Row 12: Purl 6, knit 12, purl 6.

Row 13: Knit 7, purl 10, knit 7.

Row 14: Purl 8, knit 8, purl 8.

Row 15: Knit 9, purl 6, knit 9.

Row 16: Purl 10, knit 4, purl 10.

Row 17: Knit 11, purl 2, knit 11.

Row 18: Purl all sts.

Repeat Rows 1–18 two more times. This will give you a total of 54 rows.

BO loosely and weave in ends.

Panel 3 (knit with MC)

This is the same stitch pattern as in Panel 1, but to create the mirror image, Panel 3 begins midway through the 16 row pattern where the stitches start zagging to the right.

With US 17 (12.75mm) straights (or circulars, if you prefer) and MC, CO 24 sts.

Row 1: Knit 6, RT 3 times, knit 3, RT 3 times, knit 3.

Row 2 and all WS rows (ending with Row 16): Purl.

Row 3: Knit 5, RT 3 times, knit 3, RT 3 times, knit 4.

Row 5: Knit 4, RT 3 times, knit 3, RT 3 times, knit 5.

Row 7: Knit 3, RT 3 times, knit 3, RT 3 times, knit 6.

Row 9: Knit 3, LT 3 times, knit 3, LT 3 times, knit 6.

Row 11: Knit 4, LT 3 times, knit 3, LT 3 times, knit 5.

Row 13: Knit 5, LT 3 times, knit 3, LT 3 times, knit 4.

Row 15: Knit 6, LT 3 times, knit 3, LT 3 times, knit 3.

Repeat Rows 1–16 two more times, then repeat Rows 1–6. This will give you a total of 54 rows (i.e., 16 + 16 + 16 + 6 = 54).

BO loosely and weave in ends.

Photo 2: When you are ready to seam, lay the panels in order side by side, right-side up and cast-on edges aligned. The panels shown here are unblocked. You can lightly block yours prior to sewing them together with a mattress stitch.

Making up the Blanket

Now comes the exciting part of watching your creation come together! You will likely find that your panels, with these stockinette edgings, are a little bit curly and uncooperative. Or perhaps they don't quite align perfectly. If you find your panels bothersome, you may want to lightly steam-block them to make seaming easier. To steam-block, lay the panels out flat, wrong sides up, and pin to the desired shape and dimensions. Using an iron on the steam setting, float the iron just over the surface of the fabric, forcing the steam through the fabric. If you don't have an iron handy, just spritz with water to dampen. Allow to air-dry. When you are ready to seam, lay the panels in order side by side, right-side up and cast-on edges aligned (see Photo

2). Use a mattress stitch to sew them together (see page 16 for instructions).

Adding the Border (knit with CC)

To add the border, you'll be picking up stitches along each side individually, then sewing the corners together at all 4 corners. You'll need your circulars to hold this many stitches.

With CC and circular needles, with RS facing, start in one corner. You'll be picking up 1 stitch in every row along the sides (i.e., the left and right edges if the panels are vertical), and 1 stitch in every stitch along the top and bottom, or as close to that as you can. It will still be beautiful and will still make a fine gift for the lucky recipient if you're off a few stitches, but the more stitches you can pick up and the more evenly they are distributed, the more you will preserve the elasticity of the blanket.

Row 1: Kfb of first st, knit to last st, kfb of last st.

Row 2: Knit.

Row 3: Kfb of first st, knit to last st, kfb of last st.

BO very loosely. With the tail yarn and yarn needle, sew the gaps in the corners of the border. (If you're unsure how to do this, refer to the photos on page 62 of the Birthday Wrap.) Knot and weave in ends.

Variations

There are lots of fun ways to play with this pattern, starting with just changing the colors. I've shown it here in two colorways of the same wool/cotton blend. You could also knit the entire piece in a single color with a contrasting border. I would not recommend trying to knit this with a double strand of a lighter-weight yarn. I've done it and found that the twisted stitchwork can get a little bit hairy with two strands, not to mention that it's a pain to rip back if you drop a stitch. Plus, you lose some of the stitch definition — a problem that also occurred when I tried knitting this with a thick-n-thin yarn. If you're not too concerned with your gauge being slightly different (resulting in a slightly larger or smaller blanket), consider another bulky yarn like Tahki *Montana*.

You're never too old to play with your favorite baby blanket.

LATER GATOR BLANKET

"See you later, alligator!" Now, there's a cute animal rhyme that we've all heard countless times, but probably have never seen on a baby blanket — which is exactly why I thought it would be so charming. This snappy little treasure is sure to "wow" the new parents. I've knit it with a double-strand of the softest organic cotton, making it the perfect weight for snuggling in any season. This blanket is a bit more time-consuming because of the embroidery, but so worth the extra effort for the years of crocodile smiles it will bring.

Skills Required: Picking up stitches, knitting vertical/intarsia stripes, knitting into the front and back of a stitch, crocheting a chain stitch embellishment

Size: Approx 34" x 34"

Gauge: 10 sts and 12 rows = 4"/10 cm over St st

Notes: The four color squares of this blanket are worked in stockinette stitch and are knit as a single piece. To create the color blocks, one color is worked to the middle of the row, then the opposite color is worked to the end. The color order reverses in the middle of the blanket. The border is picked up after the blanket is finished. The chain stitch embroidery is worked with a crochet hook and is easy to learn, even for beginners. The blanket as shown is knit with two strands of a worsted-weight cotton held together throughout, but you can substitute a heavier yarn and knit with a single strand if you prefer.

Glossary of Abbreviations

approx	approximately
BO	bind off
CC-1, -2	contrasting colors (1, 2)
CO	cast on
kfb/Kfb	knit into the front and back of a single stitch, increasing by 1 stitch
MC	main color
RS	right side
st(s)	stitch(es)
St st	stockinette stitch
WS	wrong side

Materials

- 2 hanks Blue Sky Alpacas *Worsted Cotton* in #638 Dandelion (150yd/137m - 3.5oz/100g; 100% organic cotton) (MC)

- 3 hanks Blue Sky Alpacas *Multi Cotton* in # 6801 Marmalade (100yd/91m - 2.4oz/67g; 100% organic cotton) (CC-1)

- 2 hanks Blue Sky Alpacas *Worsted Cotton* in #629 Ladybug (150yd/137m - 3.5oz/100g; 100% organic cotton) (CC-2 and for the crocheted lettering)

- US 15 (10mm) 24" (or longer) circular needles

- US 15 (10mm) straight needles (optional — you can use the circulars to knit the blanket back and forth)

- Scrap yarn in various colors for alligator motif (green, blue, white)

- US size J or K (6mm or 6.4mm) crochet hook

- Yarn needle

- 3 stitch markers

- Scissors

Playfully named and made of 100% organic cotton – (from left to right) Marmalade (CC-1), Ladybug (CC-2), and Dandelion (MC) by Blue Sky Alpacas.

Knitting the Later Gator Blanket

This is a simple St st blanket, but it is mildly trickier because you are knitting with two colors and changing colors in the middle of a row. Consider this blanket an easy way to dip your toes into knitting intarsia — but without the fear! When knitting intarsia, blocks of color are worked with separate balls (or bobbins) of yarn, rather than stranded across the back of the work as in fair isle knitting. For this blanket, you will be working with only two colors and there are no intricate designs — just one vertical color change in the middle of the piece. The important rule to keep in mind when changing colors in a vertical stripe (which is basically what you are doing when you change colors in the middle of each row) is that when you are ready to change colors, you have to bring the new yarn over the color you just worked, otherwise you will have an unsightly gap. This "twisting" of the yarns is always done on the WS.

To be specific, on a knit (RS) row, you will knit to the color change, then bring the old yarn in front of the new yarn — think of it as tucking the old yarn between your knitted fabric and the new yarn (see Photo 1) — then knit the next st with the new color. Similarly, on a purl (WS) row, purl to the color change, tuck in the old yarn between the new yarn and your knitted fabric, and purl the stitch in the new color (see Photo 2). Following this procedure is critical to your happiness with this project and will ensure that your stitchwork becomes one continuous piece of colorful fabric, rather than two separate and lonely vertical strips.

For this piece, all odd-numbered rows are the RS (knit) and all even-numbered rows are the WS (purl). For all rows, simply work to the color join, twisting the yarns as directed above, then complete the row in the second color.

So let's begin: With US 15 (10mm) needles and MC, CO 36 sts. With CC-1, CO 36 sts on the same needle.

Row 1 and all RS rows: With CC-1, knit 36, twisting the yarns at the color join as directed above. With MC, knit 36. Be sure to give the yarns an extra twist at the join when knitting the first row to help tighten the gap. Don't worry if this first row is a bit loose at the join. The subsequent rows are much easier to work than the first, and you can stabilize a wobbly join when you add the border later.

Row 2 and all WS rows: With MC, purl 36, twisting the yarns at the color join as directed above. With CC-1, purl 36.

Repeat Rows 1 and 2 for 25 rows. On Row 25, break CC-1 at the color join, leaving a tail to weave in later. With MC, knit 36.

Photo 1: On a knit row, you will knit to the color change, then bring the old yarn (shown in green) in front of the new yarn (shown in blue) and knit the next stitch with the new color.

Photo 2: Similarly, on a purl row, you will purl to the color change, bring the old yarn (shown in blue) in front of the new yarn (shown in green) and purl the next stitch in the new color.

Row 26: With CC-1, purl 36, twisting the yarns at the color join as directed above. With MC, purl 36.

Row 27: With MC, knit 36, twisting the yarns at the color join as directed above. With CC-1, knit 36.

Repeat Rows 26 and 27 until 50 rows are complete, ending with a purl row.

Adding the Border

To add the border, you'll be picking up stitches and knitting along all 4 sides as if they were one torturously long row, then stitching up the corner. You'll need your circulars to hold this many stitches.

With RS facing and using CC and circular needles, pick up (ideally) 1 stitch in every row on both sides and 1 stitch in every stitch along the top and bottom, placing a marker at each corner. That's 50 + 50 + 72 + 72 for 242, or as close to that as you can. It will still be beautiful and will still make a fine gift for the lucky recipient if you're off a few stitches, but the more stitches you can pick up and the more evenly they are distributed, the more you will preserve the elasticity of the blanket.

Row 1: Purl.

Row 2: Kfb first st, knit to st before next marker, kfb, slip marker, kfb, knit to st before next marker, kfb, slip marker, kfb, knit to st before next marker, kfb, slip marker, kfb, then knit to end of row.

Row 3: Knit.

Rows 4 and 5: Repeat Rows 2 and 3.

BO very loosely and weave in ends. With tail yarn, sew the gap in the corner of the border. (If you're unsure how to do this, refer to the photo on page 62 of the Birthday Wrap.) Knot and weave in ends.

Adding the Crocheted Embroidery Motifs

Now comes the fun part! You will need a crochet hook and a few yards of yarn in the weight and colors of your choice. If you're new to this nifty embellishment technique, you'll be amazed at how easy it is. Please see the photos and tutorial on page 14. I must confess that I agonized over how and where to start the lettering for this piece. I measured and fretted and pulled out several starts, thinking that it

The finished embellishment! I began with the "S" and freehanded the letters. I sketched my quirky little gator from a figurine I had in my house! To learn how to crochet an embellishment, see the tutorial on page 14.

had to be perfectly spaced. But it doesn't. It's cute no matter what you do, so skip the fretting and just start somewhere. The existing knit sts in the St st field are a good guide for keeping your crocheted stitches straight and evenly spaced if you want them to be — think of it as working on graph paper. Follow the photograph above as a guide or create your own design if you want.

Variations

If you are still wary of treading into the waters of intarsia, simply knit four individual blocks the size that you want them and sew them together. Or, similarly, knit two vertical panels with the colors in the opposite order on each and sew those together. The border directions would be the same.

If you tire easily of stockinette (and who doesn't from time to time?), then consider using moss stitch, seed stitch, or even a fun cable pattern in two of the blocks — but I would suggest keeping the embroidered blocks in stockinette to provide a smooth canvas for your chain stitching. For a personalized blanket, consider adding the child's name and a cute motif. For example, you could crochet "A is for Alex and" and then show an alligator. Want to do it in wool? Consider a solid color of Patons *Classic Wool Roving* paired with a variegated Bernat *Felting*. Have fun creating!

STARRY NIGHT BLANKET

"Star light, star bright, first star I see tonight . . ." Children of all ages are fascinated by the magic of wishing on the first evening star. Even as newborns, mine loved to drift to sleep on a twilight stroll under a pale, starry sky — perhaps making wishes of their own. What better way to tuck your little one in at night than under a starry blanket? This thick and comfy yarn is as soft as a dream and will wear well for years of bedtime stories. The chocolate/blue star stitchwork looks impressively complicated, but is actually easy enough for a beginner.

Skills Required: Passing a stitch over, backward loop cast-on, making a yarn-over

Size: Approx 24" x 34"

Gauge: 8 sts and 8 rows = 4"/10cm over St st

Notes: This blanket is knit in one piece, starting at the star stitch border at one end and finishing with the star stitch border at the opposite end. The garter stitch edges in the main portion of the blanket are incorporated into the pattern and are worked as the first and last few stitches of each row.

Glossary of Abbreviations

approx	approximately
BO	bind off
CC	contrasting color
CO	cast on
MC	main color
RS	right side
st(s)	stitch(es)
St st	stockinette stitch
WS	wrong side
yo/Yo	yarn over

* repeat instructions following the asterisk as directed

Materials

- 5 hanks Blue Sky Alpacas *Bulky* in #1211 Frost (45yd/41m - 3.5oz/100g; 50% alpaca/50% wool) (MC)

- 2 hanks Blue Sky Alpacas *Bulky* in #1006 Brown Bear (45yd/41m - 3.5oz/100g; 50% alpaca/50% wool) (CC)

- US 19 (15mm) circular needles

- Yarn needle

- Tape measure

- Scissors

- Iron (for optional steam-blocking)

- Rust-free pins (for optional steam- or spritz-blocking)

The pale twilight blue of Frost (MC) and the deep chocolate of Brown Bear (CC) are a dreamy combination — perfect for a snuggly blanket.

A fun mix of stitchwork to knit — garter, stockinette, and star stitch.

Knitting the Starry Night Blanket

You will begin by knitting the star stitch border — a simple 4-row pattern that uses 2 contrasting colors, each for 2 consecutive rows. Carry the yarn up the side for the 2 rows that you work with the opposite color. I've indicated which color to use for each row. All odd-numbered rows will be the WS; even-numbered rows will be the RS. With CC, CO 42 sts.

Row 1 (WS): With CC, purl.

Row 2 (RS): With CC, knit 2. *Yo, knit 3, pass the first of the 3 knit sts over the 2nd and 3rd sts. Repeat from * across the row, ending with knit 1.

Row 3: With MC, purl.

Row 4: With MC, knit 1. *Knit 3, pass the first of the 3 knit sts over the 2nd and 3rd sts, yo. Repeat from * across the row until last 2 sts. Knit 2, then make 1 using backward-loop cast-on.

Repeat Rows 1–4.

Row 9 (WS): With CC, purl.

Row 10 (RS): With CC, purl. Cut CC and knot. This is the last row of the star stitch border.

The main portion of the blanket begins with Row 11 and is worked with MC in St st (i.e., alternating a purl row on the WS with a knit row on the RS). Starting with Row 13, the first and last 6 sts of each row in this portion are worked in garter stitch (i.e., knit every row), so on RS rows you will just knit all the way across the row.

Row 11 (WS): With MC, purl.

Row 12 (RS): With MC, knit.

Row 13 (WS): Knit 6, purl to last 6 sts, knit 6.

Repeat Rows 12 and 13 for 50 rows, or until desired length, ending with a RS (knit) row. Then you will begin the star stitch border. Drop, but do not cut, MC.

Knitting the Opposite Border

You'll be knitting the same star stitch pattern, only the order of the colors will be reversed so they will be the mirror image of the opposite end. Remember to carry the yarn up the side for the 2 rows that you work with the opposite color.

Row 1 (WS): With CC, purl.

Row 2 (RS): With CC, purl.

Row 3: With MC, purl.

Row 4: With MC, knit 1. *Knit 3, pass the first of the 3 knit sts over the 2nd and 3rd sts, yo. Repeat from * across the row until last 2 sts. Knit 2, then make 1 using backward loop cast-on.

Row 5: With CC, purl.

Row 6: With CC, knit 2. *Yo, knit 3, pass the first of the 3 knit sts over the 2nd and 3rd sts. Repeat from * across the row, ending with knit 1.

Repeat Rows 3–6.

BO loosely purlwise and weave in all ends.

You may want to lightly steam-block your beautiful blanket to smooth out any inconsistencies at the transition between the garter stitch and star stitch borders (not that your blanket would be anything but perfect right off the needles, but just in case). To steam-block, lay the blanket out flat, wrong side up, and pin to the desired shape and dimensions. Using an iron on the steam setting, float the iron just over the surface of the fabric, forcing the steam through the fabric. If you don't have an iron handy, just spritz with water to dampen. Allow to air-dry.

Variations

If you're thinking about other ways to play with this pattern, try whipping it up in a totally unexpected colorway like hot pink and lime, or a muted palette of charcoal and dove gray. You can also work the main panel of the blanket completely in garter stitch, or use your favorite combination of stitches. If you're looking to make this blanket a different width, keep in mind that the star stitch border requires a multiple of 3 stitches.

COCOONS & PODS

Time for snuggling!

Peek-a-Boo Pod

Eskimo Kiss Hooded Cocoon

Tab Top Cocoon

Ribbons & Bows Cocoon

Ho Ho Ho! Cocoon & Hat

Snuggle Me Nursing Cocoon

PEEK-A-BOO POD

Newborns love the snug feeling of being curled in the womb, and this knitted pod is sure to lull them happily to dreamland. This piece is perfect for newborns and especially their parents who want to capture an image of their peacefully resting baby. If you have mastered knitting in the round, you'll be amazed at how fast this piece will come together. Using a bulky yarn and your size 19s, you can cast on this project in the morning, bind off before lunch.

Skills Required: Knitting in the round on circular needles, knitting 2 stitches together

Size: Fits newborns up to 10 lbs/21"; finished piece measures approx 12" deep and 12" wide

Gauge: Approx 8 sts and 10 rows = 4"/10cm over St st

Notes: Babies much older than 14 days or so, regardless of their size, don't always want to curl up as much as the brand new ones do, so this piece is best suited for the newly born.

Glossary of Abbreviations

approx	approximately
BO	bind off
CC	contrasting color
CO	cast on
dec	decrease/decreasing
k2tog	knit 2 stitches together
MC	main color
rem	remaining
st(s)	stitch(es)
St st	stockinette stitch

* repeat instructions following the asterisk as directed

Materials

- 1 skein Aslan Trends *Del Sur* in #138 Purple (87yd/80m - 3.5oz/100g; 100% wool) (MC)

- 1 skein Colorful Nest *Whimsical* in Forest Nymph (50yd/46m - 3.5oz/100g; 65% mohair/35% wool) (CC)

- US 19 (15 mm) 24" circular needles

- Stitch marker or scrap yarn

- Tape measure

- Yarn needle

- Scissors

- Approx 2½ yards of ½" satin ribbon (optional and not shown)

The rich jewel tones of Colorful Nest Whimsical in Forest Nymph (CC) and the deep plum of Aslan Trends Del Sur #138 Purple (MC) are a sumptuous combination that works well for either a boy or a girl.

A warm and colorful palette for fall to try — Feza Yarns Platino in 001 as CC and Malabrigo Gruesa in #96 Sunset for MC.

Knitting the Peek-a-boo Pod

With CC, CO 40 sts. Place marker and join to knit in the round, being careful not to twist sts.

Knit 4 rounds with CC (or 1 more if you prefer a wider, chunkier border). Cut CC and join MC.

Knit 18 rounds in MC, then begin dec sequence as follows:

Round 19: *Knit 8, k2tog. Repeat from * to end of round.

Round 20: *Knit 7, k2tog. Repeat from * to end of round.

Round 21: Knit.

Round 22: *Knit 6, k2tog. Repeat from * to end of round.

Round 23: *Knit 5, k2tog. Repeat from * to end of round.

Round 24: Knit.

Round 25: *Knit 4, k2tog. Repeat from * to end of round.

Round 26: *Knit 3, k2tog. Repeat from * to end of round.

Cut yarn, leaving a 12" tail. Thread yarn through needle and tie off sts. Weave in all ends.

Adding Final Touches

If you like, you can weave ribbon through the border of MC and CC and tie it in a bow, or even knit an I-cord (see page 34). In Photo 1 I've shown a few strands of yarn used as a bow.

Photo 1: Weave your choice of a yarn (shown) or satin ribbon drawstring through stitches where the border (knit in the contrasting color) meets the main color.

If you'll be using this pod frequently, such as for a photography prop, I suggest adding a hidden drawstring to do the "work" of supporting the baby in position so your decorative ribbon or yarn bow (should you decide to add it) won't get stretched and wrinkled. To do this, thread an extra piece of MC through the border of MC and CC and cut, leaving enough ribbon or yarn to tie a bow.

Variations

Looking for other ideas? You could easily knit the Peek-a-Boo Pod in another gorgeous combination such as thick-n-thin Malabrigo *Gruesa* or *Aquarella* as the MC, paired with the wonderful textures of Feza Yarns *Platino* as the border (see photo on page 91). Or experiment with your favorite novelty yarns as the border. Anything that provides a textural contrast would be just as fun! Just be sure to check your gauge when substituting yarns.

ESKIMO KISS HOODED COCOON

Picture yourself nose to nose for an Eskimo kiss with your sweet little tidbit bundled up in this cozy hooded cocoon/snuggler. It knits up in a breeze on 19s and can be a nice weekend project for an adventuresome beginner, or whipped out in an afternoon by a more experienced knitter. The Eskimo Kiss features an invisible drawstring tucked under the playful border and another at the toes, making diaper changes a snap and giving you complete control over how much skin you want exposed.

Skills Required: Knitting in the round on circular needles, knitting 2 stitches together, picking up stitches, backward loop cast-on

Size: Fits newborns 5–8 lbs/19" (8–10 lbs/22"); finished piece measures approx 18" long (22") and 14–16" (16–18") in circumference at chest and is quite stretchy

Gauge: Approx 8 sts and 10 rows = 4"/10cm over St st

Notes: This cocoon is knit in one piece from the top down. The hood is knit flat (on your preference of circular or straight needles), then additional stitches are cast on around the base of the hood to join in the round for the body of the cocoon. After the hood is sewn together at the crown, the border is picked up and knit in the round.

Glossary of Abbreviations

approx	approximately
BO	bind off
CC	contrasting color
CO	cast on
dec	decrease/decreasing
k2tog	knit 2 stitches together
MC	main color
rem	remaining
RS	right side
st(s)	stitch(es)
St st	stockinette stitch
WS	wrong side

Materials

- 2 skeins Aslan Trends *Los Andes* in #1332 Pink Mist or #1331 Alaska Blues (87yd/80m - 3.5oz/100g; 85% merino wool/15% polyamide) (MC)

- 1 skein Colorful Nest *Whimsical* in Garden (for pink) or Sea Glass (for blue) (50 yd/46m - 3.5oz/100g; 65% mohair/35% wool) (CC)

- US 19 (15mm) circular needles

- US 19 (15mm) straight needles (optional — you can knit the hood back and forth on circulars if you prefer)

- Stitch marker or scrap yarn (two colors)

- Tape measure

- Yarn needle

- Scissors

- Approx 2 yards of ½" satin ribbon (optional and not shown)

The cool hues of Aslan Trends Los Andes in #1331 Alaska Blues (MC shown at right) and Colorful Nest Whimsical in Sea Glass (CC) are a calming combination.

Bright and vibrant Aslan Trends Los Andes in #1332 Pink Mist (MC shown at right) combines well with Colorful Nest Whimsical in Garden (CC).

Knitting the Eskimo Kiss Hooded Cocoon

We will begin by knitting the hood, which is knit flat and then seamed at the crown later. With US 19 (15mm) straights or circulars, CO 14 (20) sts, leaving a 12" tail for sewing hood later.

Row 1: Knit.

Row 2: Purl.

Repeat Rows 1 and 2 (stockinette stitch) until you have completed 11 (13) rows, ending with a knit row. This will set you up to knit (rather than purl) in the round for the cocoon. If you were using straight needles, transfer your sts to US 19 (15mm) circular needles to begin working in the round. Using the backward loop method (see Photo 1), CO an additional 10 sts for a total of 24 (30). Place marker and join to knit in the round, making sure stitches are not twisted. The remainder of the cocoon will be knit in the round.

For smaller newborn size, knit until piece measures 18" from the top (or until desired length). The smaller newborn size has no dec.

Follow instructions for finishing below.

For larger size, knit until piece measures 20" from the top (or until desired length), then begin dec sequence as follows:

Round 1: Knit 10, k2tog (i.e., at your midpoint marker at the back of the piece).

Round 2: Knit 9, k2tog.

Round 3: Knit 8, k2tog.

Round 4: Knit 7, k2tog.

Round 5: Knit 6, k2tog.

Round 6: Knit 5, k2tog.

Finishing

Knot and weave in ends, or, if you want to have an opening for the toes at the bottom, leave a longer tail and knot the end to use as a drawstring. If you decide to do this, make sure your knot is big enough and the tail is long enough that you don't end up

with a beautiful cocoon gracefully unraveling itself at the bottom because your knot slipped right through the stitches. Cut yarn to desired length and use a needle to pull yarn through the rem sts.

Photo 1: This is the Backward Loop CO. After you finish your 11 (13) rows, transfer your stitches to your circular needles. With the knit side facing you, hold the work in your right hand and make a simple loop with the working yarn, as shown in the photo, and place it on the needle. You just added 1 stitch! Continue looping yarn around in this manner until you have added 8 (10) more stitches, making sure that the working yarn is always between the stitch you just added and the previous stitch (rather than in front of the stitch you just added). From here you are ready to place your marker, join, and knit in the round.

Photo 2: To create the hood, simply fold it in half and with WS facing each other, sew along the CO edge using the tail yarn. Tuck in the tail, knot it, and weave it in.

Sewing the Hood

To create the hood, thread the tail yarn of your CO edge through a yarn needle. Fold the hood and with WS facing each other, sew the hood together along the CO edge (see Photo 2). I like to sew it from the outside (i.e., the RS), rather than turn it inside out, so I can make sure that the seam is coming along as invisibly as possible.

The Border

There is always more than one way to skin a cat, or in this case, knit it a cocoon. Here are a couple of things to consider before you get to work on the border: First, are you making this for normal wear or for a limited use such as a photo shoot or special outing? If it is the former, then you can consider these options: replace the border yarn I've used here with something less "fluffy" that still suits your needs; add only 1 row of border rather than the 2 rows in the instructions below; or just skip the border entirely, which means you're finished!

Next, decide whether you want the purl (i.e., "bumpy") side showing around the face, or the knit (i.e., "flat") side. Personally, I prefer the purl side to show, to add to the textural interest. Besides, there is the bonus that the purl side tends to want to curl outward and away from the face like a flower blossom (rather than curling inward, which can be a bit cavelike).

So to pick up and knit the border as I've shown here (with the purl side showing around the face), you'll be picking up the stitches from the RS and knitting in the round. With the RS facing out, pick up a stitch by going through the RS of the knitted fabric, placing the new stitch on your needle, and bringing the needle with the new stitch through to the RS.

Three colorways of the Eskimo Kiss Cocoon — the first in Aslan Trends Los Andes *in Alaska Blues and Colorful Nest* Whimsical *in Sea Glass; the second in* Los Andes *in Pink Mist with* Whimsical *in Garden; and the third (at far right) in Aslan Trends* Del Sur *in Azul del Sur #14, with the border in* Whimsical *in Sea Glass.*

Pick up approx 26 (30) stitches around the opening, or even a few more if you tend to knit rather tightly. Whatever you do, don't chintz on picking up the stitches or your border will look more like a little tunnel with the baby's face way at the bottom. You're almost there:

Place marker and knit 2 rounds.

BO very loosely (again, beware of the tunnel) and weave in ends.

If you prefer the knit side showing, simply turn your piece inside-out and, with the WS facing, pick up your stitches by going through the WS, placing the stitch on the needle, and drawing the needle with the new stitch through to the WS. Pick up your 30 stitches and follow the same instructions as above.

You can add another touch of color by weaving a satin ribbon, I-cord, yarn, or other embellishment through the holes in the fabric around the opening. Tie a bow and admire your handiwork!

Variations

Don't let the image of frosty Eskimos in fur-lined parkas influence you! You can play with the gauge and easily knit this up in a nice cotton such as *I Am Allergic to Wool* by Farmhouse Yarns for those summer babies. For a different and equally fun border, try Farmhouse Yarns *Trixie's Loopy Mohair*.

TAB TOP COCOON

Button up your bundle of joy in this Tab Top Cocoon! This delicate little piece will keep your sweet pea cozy and happy for his or her first introduction to family and friends at the Sip and See. The interesting woven texture of the upper band offers a subtle textural contrast to the silky smooth brushed suri alpaca of the base. If you're looking to try something more challenging than stockinette or garter stitch, you'll be pleased with how easily you'll master the twisted stitches used in the band. Choose a button for the tab top to suit your taste!

Skills Required: Knitting in the round on circular needles, knitting 2 stitches together, slipping a stitch, slip knit pass decrease, picking up stitches, and knitting into the back of a stitch

Size: Fits newborns 5–8 lbs/19" (8–10 lbs/22"); finished piece measures approximately 16" long (20") and 14–16" (16–18") in circumference at chest and is quite stretchy

Gauge: Not critical for top band; 12 sts and 12 rows = 4"/10cm over St st

Notes: The upper band of this cocoon is knit as a long strip, which is tapered by decreasing to form the tab portion that will fold over and button. The band is then sewn together (leaving the tab free) to form the top opening of the cocoon. The bottom of the cocoon is knit by picking up stitches around the band and knitting in the round for the desired length. You can adjust the width of this piece by simply taking your desired opening size, knitting a band that length, then continuing with the decreases for the tab.

Glossary of Abbreviations

approx	approximately
BO	bind off
CC-1, -2	contrasting colors (1, 2)
CO	cast on
dec	decrease/decreasing
k2tog	knit 2 stitches together
MC	main color
rem	remaining
RS	right side
skp/Skp	slip knit pass (also known as slip 1, knit 1, pass the slipped stitch over or sl1, k1, psso)
st(s)	stitch(es)
St st	stockinette stitch
WS	wrong side

Materials

- 1 skein Blue Sky Alpacas *Brushed Suri* in #904 Fudgesicle (142yd/130m - 1.76oz/50g; 67% baby suri/22% merino/11% bamboo) (MC)

- 1 ball Classic Elite *Katydid* in #7319 Chintz Pink (90yd/87m - 1.76oz/50g; 100% organic cotton) (CC-1)

- 1 hank Berroco *Seduce* in #4492 Trance (100yd/92m - 1.41oz/40g; 47% rayon/25% linen/17% silk/11% nylon) (CC-2)

- US 15 (10mm) 28" (or smaller) circular needles

- US 15 (10mm) straight needles (optional — you can knit the top band back and forth on circulars if you prefer)

- Stitch marker or scrap yarn

- Yarn needle

- Tape measure

- Button (small enough to fit through finished stitches, as the pattern does not include a buttonhole)

A soft and feminine combination of Classic Elite Katydid in Chintz Pink (CC-1), Berroco Seduce in Trance (CC-2), and Blue Sky Alpacas Brushed Suri in Fudgesicle (MC).

The organic hues of Katydid in #7377 Perfect Storm (CC-1), Berroco Seduce in #4437 Gris-Bleu (CC-2), and Be Sweet Brushed Mohair in Dark Camel (CC-3) are perfect for a boy or a girl.

Knitting the Tab Top Band

You'll jump right into a very short (but complex-sounding) 2-row pattern. Pay close attention to whether you "slip" vs. "skip" the stitches — this piece calls for both. To refresh you, "skip" means leave that stitch on the left needle and just ignore it until otherwise instructed. "Slip" means to slip the stitch purlwise (i.e., as if to purl it) from the left needle onto the right needle without working it. You'll be slipping stitches later when decreasing for the tab portion of the band.

Also, this pattern calls for two types of decreases: k2tog (i.e., knit 2 stitches together) and skp (i.e., slip 1 stitch, knit the next stitch, then pass the slipped stitch over the knit stitch — also known in abbreviated terms as sl1, k1, psso). A quick word about these stitches — they are nearly mirror images of each other, meaning the k2tog slants to the right and the skp slants to the left. As you can imagine, it is quite handy to know how to do both, especially when you want something to evenly taper like the tab at the end of this band. If you have mastered k2tog, you can easily learn the skp and it will change your knitting life. You'll wonder how you managed to go this long knitting so many lopsided things that only ever slanted to the right.

The skp is done just as it sounds: slip the first stitch purlwise (i.e., as if to purl it) from the left needle to the right needle, then knit the next stitch as you normally would, then lift the slipped stitch over the stitch you just knit and pull it off the needle — just as if you were binding off one stitch (which, in effect, you have just done). You can see that the slipped stitch that you pulled off the needle is now "pointing" (or slanting) to the left — and there's your left slanting decrease.

Another thing I want to mention about this pattern stitch that's used in the band — it is extremely stretchy width-wise! Those 12 stitches you'll cast on can go from about 2 inches wide to more than 4 inches wide if you like. Stretch it out along the way and see how wide you prefer it, then use that to gauge how long you want your band to be (remember, the length of the band is the width of the opening) before you start the decreases for the tab.

So, with all of that out of the way, let's get to knitting this cocoon!

With US 15 (10mm) straights (or circulars if you prefer) and 1 strand each of CC-1 and CC-2 held together, CO 12 sts for either size cocoon, leaving a 12" tail for sewing band together later. Begin the pattern st:

Row 1 and all RS rows: Skip the first st and from back of left needle, insert needle in back loop of second st on left needle, knit (i.e., knit the second st through the back loop) and leave on needle; knit the first st through front loop, then slip both sts from needle together. Repeat to end of row.

Row 2 and all WS rows: Skip first st, purl the second st and leave on needle; then purl the skipped st and slip both sts from needle together. Repeat to end of row.

Work this pattern st for 50 (56) rows, which is approx 17" (20"), or for your desired width for the top of your cocoon. End with a purl (WS) row so you can begin the dec on a knit (RS) row.

Begin dec for the tab and continue to work Row 2 on all WS rows:

Row 1: Skp, knit 8, k2tog (10 sts rem).

Row 3: Skp, knit 6, k2tog (8 sts rem).

Row 5: Skp, knit 4, k2tog (6 sts rem).

Row 7: Skp, knit 2, k2tog (4 sts rem).

Row 9: Knit.

BO and weave in ends.

Photo 1: The mirrored decreases form a neat taper at the tip of the band. Place your button where it will nicely secure the folded tab.

Photo 2: The finished Tab Top Cocoon!

Finishing the Band

Thread the CO tail yarns with a yarn needle and with RS facing out, fold the band to your desired width and sew the band closed (see Photo 1), leaving the tab free to fold over the front of the band. I sewed the one in the photo at the row before I began the dec, which was about 17". Affix the button, as shown in Photo 2, or wherever you like.

Knitting the Cocoon

With US 15 (10mm) circulars and MC, pick up 32 (38) sts around the bottom edge of the band.

Knit 38 (44) rounds or until desired length (the one shown in the photos here is the smaller size and measures approx 11" from the bottom of the band to the bottom of the cocoon) or 14" total.

Cut yarn and pull yarn through sts to close.

Knot and weave in end.

Variations

The tab top band of this cocoon knits up easily in other tape or ribbon yarns, which seem to show off this particular stitch used for the band quite well. And you don't have to use a second yarn in the band. I chose to use these two because I liked the little hint of shimmer and different weight and texture that the *Seduce* offered against the wider, matte tape of the *Katydid*. You can also try Berroco *Origami*, Tahki *Good Earth Cotton*, or any of the beautiful colors of hand-dyed satin ribbon offered by Hanah Silks or Judi & Co. For the base, you might consider *Brushed Mohair* by Be Sweet.

RIBBONS & BOWS COCOON

I love the simplicity of this bow-bedecked little number — a basic, easy-to-knit cocoon shape, with a sweet little knot at the toes and beautiful hand-dyed ribbon for textural contrast. Perfect for introducing your tiny new addition to the rest of the family. This is a very versatile and gender-neutral piece that you can whip up in whatever combination suits you. This would also make a sweet addition to any newborn photographer's box of goodies.

Skills Required: Knitting in the round on circular needles, knitting on double-pointed needles, knitting 2 stitches together, knitting an I-cord

Size: Fits newborns 5–7 lbs/19" (7–9 lbs/22"); finished piece measures approx 16" (17") in circumference and 15" (17") in length before I-cord

Gauge: 9 sts and 10 rows = 4"/10cm over St st

Notes: This cocoon is knit in the round, with 3 stripes of ribbon knit as a second yarn. From the top, the yarn stripes are 9, 7, and 5 stitches wide, respectively. The bows are tied on separately.

Glossary of Abbreviations

approx	approximately
BO	bind off
CC	contrasting color
CO	cast on
dec	decrease
k2tog/K2tog	knit 2 stitches together
MC	main color
st(s)	stitch(es)
St st	stockinette stitch

* repeat instructions following the asterisk as directed

Materials

- 2 skeins Tahki Stacy Charles *Mia* in #008 Coffee (41yd/38m - 1.75oz/50g; 100% cotton) (MC)
- 5 yds Judi & Co. ½" rayon ribbon in Dirty Denim (CC)
- US 17 (12.75mm) 26" (or smaller) circular needles
- US 17 (12.75mm) set of double-pointed needles
- Stitch marker or scrap yarn
- Yarn needle
- Tape measure
- Scissors

A perfect duo for welcoming a sweet baby boy — rayon ribbon in Dirty Denim by Judi & Co and Mia in #008 Coffee by Tahki Stacy Charles.

Fun for a Valentine's or Christmas baby, hand-dyed American Beauty silk ribbon by Hanah Silk is paired with Mia in #007 Natural by Tahki Stacy Charles.

For the ivory cocoon shown here, I added 3 extra bows of Hanah Silk hand-dyed silk ribbon in brilliant American Beauty along the left side of the cocoon. As with any silk or other delicate fabric, this piece should be dry-cleaned.

Knitting the Ribbons & Bows Cocoon

With US 17 (12.75mm) circulars and MC, CO 30 (32) sts. Place marker and join to knit in the round, taking care not to twist sts.

Knit 10 rounds.

Round 11: Drop MC and with CC, knit 9 stitches loosely, carrying MC behind work; cut and knot CC and with MC, knit to end of round.

Knit 4 rounds.

Round 16: Knit 1, then drop MC and with CC, knit 7 stitches loosely, carrying MC behind work; cut and knot CC and with MC, knit to end of round.

Knit 4 rounds.

Round 21: Knit 2, then drop MC and with CC, knit 5 stitches loosely, carrying MC behind work; cut and knot CC and with MC, knit to end of round.

Knit 5 (7) rounds, then begin dec sequence as follows. Change to double-pointed needles when you have too few sts to work on circulars.

Round 1: *Knit 8 (6), k2tog. Repeat from * to end of round.

Round 2: Knit.

Round 3: *Knit 7 (5), k2tog. Repeat from * to end of round.

Round 4: Knit.

Round 5: *Knit 6 (4), k2tog. Repeat from * to end of round.

Knit 5 (6) more rounds.

Round 10 (11): *Knit 4 (3), k2tog. Repeat from * to end of round.

FOR SMALLER NEWBORN SIZE:

Begin I-cord by moving all sts to 1 double-pointed needle, then:

Row 1: Knit.

Row 2: *Knit 2, k2tog. Repeat from * to end of row.

Row 3: *Knit 1, k2tog. Repeat from * to end of row.

Rows 4–7: Knit.

BO and weave in ends. (Your cocoon should look like Photo 1 on page 109). Tie I-cord in a knot at bottom of cocoon (see Photo 2 on page 109).

FOR LARGER NEWBORN SIZE:

Round 12: Knit.

Round 13: *Knit 2, k2tog. Repeat from * to end of row.

Round 14: Knit.

Round 15: *Knit 1, k2tog. Repeat from * to end of row.

Round 16: Knit.

Round 17: *Knit 1, k2tog. Repeat from * to end of row.

Round 18: Knit.

Begin I-cord by moving all sts to 1 double-pointed needle, then:

Rows 1–2: Knit.

Row 3: K2tog, knit 6, k2tog.

Row 4: Knit.

Row 5: K2tog, knit 4, k2tog.

Rows 6–9: Knit.

Row 10: K2tog across the row.

BO and weave in ends. (Your cocoon should look like Photo 1 on page 109.) Tie I-cord in a knot at bottom of cocoon (see Photo 2 on page 109).

Adding the Ribbon Bows

Decide how many ribbon bows you want and where you want to place them. You may need to lightly iron your ribbon, but check the care label before you do. Depending on my mood, I'll either place 3 bows — one at the end of each of the ribbon stripes, or 6 bows — one on each end of each ribbon stripe (as shown on page 106). Tie your piece of ribbon in place and make your bow (see Photo 3).

Variations

If you want to stick with cotton as I've shown here, you can also try *I Am Allergic to Wool* by Farmhouse Yarns, or it would have a totally different look knit with a thick-n-thin wool like Aslan Trends *Del Sur* — just be sure to check your gauge. You can really make a statement with this piece depending on the width of your ribbon. I've used up to 1½" wide ribbon and it turned out very pretty. And don't limit yourself to just bows for the final touch — consider using a narrower width of your ribbon and make a few small, fringey tassels. Or use your ribbon to knit some petite flowers and place them at the ends of the ribbon stripes.

Photo 1: The Ribbons & Bows Cocoon right off the needles. You're ready for the finishing touches.

Photo 2: Tie a knot at the toes.

Photo 3: Slip a length of ribbon under the ribbon stitch as shown, and tie your bows.

HO HO HO! COCOON & HAT

Celebrate the season and the arrival of your little one with this merry Ho Ho Ho! Cocoon and matching hat set. Both pieces are adorned with a fluffy yarn around the border and finished off with a snowy pom-pom. The cocoon is knit in a ribbed stitch bodice that frames the fun embroidered motifs. I'm showing it here in two festive variations and hope it inspires you to add a design of your own. This is a straightforward and easy knit on 15s, and it is just as cute if you prefer not to add the embroidery.

Skills Required: Knitting in the round on circular needles, knitting in the round with double-pointed needles, crocheting a chain stitch embellishment, making a pom-pom

Size: Cocoon fits newborns up to 8 lbs/21" (12 lbs/23"); finished piece measures 16" (18") in circumference and 16" (19") long. Hat fits newborns up to 14" head size

Gauge: 9 sts and 14 rows = 4"/10cm over St st

Notes: This is an easy cocoon that is knit from the top down in the round on circular needles, with minimal shaping — just a few decreases on double-pointed needles at the very bottom of the cocoon. The crocheted chain stitch embroidery for the motifs is worked with a crochet hook and is easy to learn, even for beginners. The hat is also a simple knit on double-pointed needles, with a chunky stocking tip before the pom-pom.

Glossary of Abbreviations

approx	approximately
BO	bind off
CC	contrasting color
CO	cast on
dec	decrease/decreasing
k2tog	knit 2 stitches together
MC	main color
st(s)	stitch(es)
St st	stockinette stitch

* repeat instructions following the asterisk as directed

Materials

- 3 balls Debbie Bliss *Como* in #18 Pear (46yd/42m - 1.76oz/50g; 90% wool/10% cashmere) (MC)
- 1 ball Tahki *Natasha* in #01 Cream (38yd/35m - 1.75oz/50g; 38% wool/32% acrylic/24% alpaca/5%nylon) (CC)
- Few yards of scrap yarn for crocheted embroidery — shown is Debbie Bliss *Como* in #12 Red
- US 15 (10mm) circular needles
- US 15 (10mm) set of double-pointed needles
- Size J or K crochet hook
- Stitch marker or scrap yarn
- Tape measure
- Scissors

Fluffy white Natasha by Tahki (CC) lends a jolly accent to Como by Debbie Bliss in #18 Pear (MC above left) and #23 Blue (MC above right).

Knitting the Ho Ho Ho! Cocoon

With CC and US 15 (10mm) circular needles, CO 32 (36) sts. Place marker and join to knit in the round, taking care not to twist sts.

For border: Purl 4 rounds with CC. Cut CC.

For band of St st: With MC, knit in the round (creating St st) for 3 ½". Purl 1 round to mark the end of the band of St st and the beginning of the ribbed bodice. This field of St st will provide a nice, flat canvas for your embroidery, so if you think you need more space for your designs, you can easily add as many rounds as you like. Just remember to work fewer rounds of the ribbed bodice if you want the cocoon to still be the same length.

For ribbed bodice: *Knit 3, purl 1. Repeat from * until ribbed bodice measures 9½" (11½") or approx 13½" (15½") from top of the piece. Purl 1 round to mark the end of the ribbed bodice and the beginning of the tip.

A quick note here: If you are planning to add an embroidered motif to your cocoon, do not begin your decreases just yet. You will find it much easier to work the embroidery if you have wide access to the inside of the cocoon from the top and the bottom. Skip now to the ***Adding the crocheted embroidery motifs*** section below. When you are finished with the embellishments, continue with the tip:

For tip: Knit 6 (8) rounds, then begin dec sequence as follows, transferring your sts to US 15 (10mm) double-pointed needles as needed:

*Knit 6 (7), k2tog. Repeat from * to end of round.

*Knit 5 (6), k2tog. Repeat from * to end of round.

*Knit 4 (5), k2tog. Repeat from * to end of round.

*Knit 3 (4), k2tog. Repeat from * to end of round.

*Knit 2 (3), k2tog. Repeat from * to end of round.

Cut MC and pull tail through remaining sts. Knot and weave in ends. Pull fluffy nubs of *Natasha* through to outside of cocoon. Add a pom-pom if you like (see instructions on page 17).

This toasty Let it Snow! variation knit with Como in #23 Blue is perfect for a wintery welcome.

Photo 1: To crochet the lettering, begin by inserting your crochet hook into the first stitch above the purl row and work upward. Use the existing rows and columns of knit stitches as a guide. If you need some pointers on this technique, see the tutorial on page 14.

Adding the Crocheted Embroidery Motifs

Now comes the fun part! You will need a crochet hook and a few yards of yarn in the weight and color(s) of your choice. If you're new to this nifty embellishment technique, you'll be amazed at how easy it is. Please see the brief tutorial on page 14. For the "Ho Ho Ho," begin by inserting your crochet hook in the first st above the first purl row (see Photo 1). The existing knit sts in the St st field are a good guide for keeping your crocheted stitches straight and evenly spaced — think of it as working on graph paper. For the long vertical lines of the H's, I followed the vertical rows of knit sts from the purl row to just under the border at the top. For the horizontal lines of the H's, I followed a horizontal row of knit sts. I free-handed the O's, using the grid of the St st field as a guide. For the snowflakes, follow the photograph as a guide or create your own snowflake if you want. When you are finished with the embroidery, continue with instructions for the tip as directed above.

Knitting the Ho Ho Ho! Hat

With CC and US 15 (10mm) circular needles, CO 26 sts. Place marker and join to knit in the round, taking care not to twist sts.

Round 1: Knit.

Round 2: Purl.

Round 3: Knit. Cut CC.

With MC, continue knitting all rounds until piece measures 5" from CO edge, then begin dec sequence as follows:

Round 1: *Knit 4, k2tog. Repeat from * to end of round, ending k2tog.

Round 2: Knit.

Round 3: *Knit 3, k2tog. Repeat from * to end of round, ending knit1.

Round 4: Knit.

Round 5: *Knit 2, k2tog. Repeat from * to end of round, ending knit1.

Rounds 6–8: Knit.

Round 9: *Knit 1, k2tog. Repeat from * to end of round, ending knit1.

Rounds 10–13: Knit.

Break MC and pull tail through remaining sts. Knot and weave in ends. Pull fluffy nubs of *Natasha* through to outside of hat. Add a pom-pom if you like (see page 17).

Variations

This basic cocoon and hat pattern will work well for any occasion or any season. You can experiment with other colors, unusual border yarns, chunky cables instead of the ribbing, or your own embroidery ideas — a perky XOXO motif would be perfectly kissable for a boy or a girl. A bright yellow hat and cocoon with a little bee buzzing around the top is a cheery way for a springtime baby to make an entrance. Consider a flirty little novelty yarn to replace the tufted *Natasha* for the border. For the cocoon, Patons *Classic Wool Roving* offers a wide palette of rich solids, and Bernat *Felting* comes in a beautiful selection of mottled color combinations. Just be sure to check your gauge when substituting yarns.

Holidays cocoons for wintertime snuggling! The blue Let it Snow! variation at left is knit in the larger size.

SNUGGLE ME NURSING COCOON

As a nursing mom myself, I designed this piece for moms who want a bit of privacy for nursing, but are looking for something more stylish than a flannel blanket to toss over themselves. This nursing cocoon offers just that! The cover-up is knit in seed stitch on 17s, so it is pretty on both sides for tossing over your shoulder, and it's airy enough to offer a comfortable covering for baby snuggled down in the cocoon.

Skills Required: Knitting in the round on circular needles, knitting in the round on double-pointed needles, backward loop cast-on, knitting 2 stitches together

Size: Fits newborns up to 12 lbs/24"; finished cover-up is approx 27" wide and 13" long; cocoon is approx 17" in circumference and 18" long

Gauge: 8 sts and 12 rows = 4"/10cm over St st

Notes: This piece is knit in one piece from the top edge of the cover-up to the bottom of the cocoon. The cover-up portion is knit flat, then additional stitches are cast on to knit the cocoon in the round.

Glossary of Abbreviations

approx	approximately
BO	bind off
CC-1, -2	contrasting colors (1, 2)
CO	cast on
k2tog	knit 2 stitches together
MC	main color
st(s)	stitch(es)
St st	stockinette stitch

* repeat instructions following the asterisk as directed

Materials

- 2 skeins Araucania *Coliumo* in #6 Magenta (95yd/87m - 3.5oz/100g; 70% wool/30% silk) (MC)

- 1 skein Kitchen Sink Dyeworks *Merino Silk Worsted* in Poppi (240yd/219m - 4oz/117g; 60% merino wool/40% silk) (CC-1)

- 1 skein Farmhouse Yarns *Lumpy Bumpy* in Zinnias (150yd/137m - 4oz/117g; 99% merino wool/1% nylon) (CC-2)

- US 17 (12.75mm) 26" (or smaller) circular needles

- US 17 (12.75mm) double-pointed needles

- Stitch marker or scrap yarn

- Tape measure

- Scissors

Araucania vivid Coliumo in #6 Magenta (MC) is beautifully complemented by Kitchen Sink Dyeworks Merino Silk Worsted in Poppi (CC-1 at bottom) and multi-toned Farmhouse Yarns Lumpy Bumpy in Zinnias (CC-2 at top).

Aslan Trends Del Sur in #1 White (MC) is richly accented with Malabrigo Merino Worsted in #27 Bobby Blue (CC-1 at bottom) and the variegated hues of Farmhouse Yarns Lumpy Bumpy in Kaleidoscope (CC-2 at top).

Knitting the Snuggle Me Nursing Cocoon

THE COVER-UP

You'll begin at the top edge of the cover-up portion of the cocoon. This is a rectangle that is knit flat. After you work the first 2 rows, you'll begin a 6-row pattern consisting of 2 rows of St st worked with CC-1 and CC-2 held together, and 4 rows of seed st worked with MC. Be sure to carry the nonworking yarns neatly up the side.

With MC and US 17 circular needles, CO 48 sts.

Row 1: *Knit 1, purl 1. Repeat from * across the row.

Row 2: *Purl 1, knit 1. Repeat from * across the row. These 2 rows make up seed st, where you knit the purl sts and purl the knit sts.

Row 3: With CC-1 and CC-2 held together, knit across the row.

Row 4: Purl.

Row 5: With MC, * knit 1, purl 1. Repeat from * across the row.

Row 6: *Purl 1, knit 1. Repeat from * across the row.

Row 7: *Knit 1, purl 1. Repeat from * across the row (i.e., repeat Row 5).

Row 8: *Purl 1, knit 1. Repeat from * across the row (i.e., repeat Row 6).

Repeat Rows 3–8 until you have worked a total of 35 rows (approx 13"), or until your desired length, ending on an odd-numbered (i.e., purl side of St st) row. Cut CC-1 and CC-2.

With MC, BO 18 sts, purl 12 sts, then BO the remaining 18 sts and cut MC. You should have 12 live sts in the middle of the row remaining on your needle (see Photo 1).

With the purl side of the St st facing up, reattach MC to the first live st at the right of the end and CO an additional 23 sts using the backward loop method (see Photo 2). You should have a total of 35 sts. If you are unfamiliar with this CO method, don't worry! Check the quick explanation in the Eskimo Kiss Hooded Cocoon pattern (page 96).

Place marker and join to knit in the round, taking care not to twist sts. You are now ready to begin knitting the cocoon!

Knitting the cover-up in the alternate colorway of White, Bobby Blue, and Kaleidoscope (yarns shown on page 117).

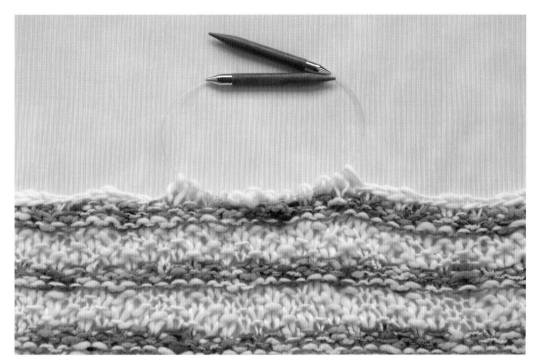

Photo 1: After you BO the outer 18 stitches on each side of the last row of the cover-up, you'll have 12 live stitches remaining on your needle. You are ready to CO for the cocoon.

Photo 2: With the purl side of the stockinette stitch facing up, reattach MC to the first live stitch at the right of the end and CO an additional 23 stitches using the backward loop method.

THE COCOON

Be sure to carry the non-working yarns neatly inside the cocoon.

Rounds 1–4: With MC, knit.

Rounds 5–6: With CC-1 and CC-2, knit.

Rounds 7–10: With MC, knit.

Rounds 11–12: With CC-1 and CC-2, knit.

Round 13–16: *Knit 1, purl 1. Repeat from * around, creating seed st.

Round 17: With CC-1 and CC-2, knit to last 2 sts, then k2tog (34 sts remain).

Round 18: With CC-1 and CC-2, knit.

Rounds 19–22: With MC, knit.

Rounds 23–24: With CC-1 and CC-2, knit.

Rounds 25–32: With MC, knit.

Rounds 33–34: With CC-1 and CC-2, knit. Cut CC-1 and CC-2.

Round 35: With MC, *knit 6, k2tog. Repeat from * around, end knit 2.

Round 36: Knit.

Round 37: *Knit 5, k2tog. Repeat from * around, end knit 2.

Round 38: Knit.

Round 39: *Knit 4, k2tog. Repeat from * around, end knit 2.

Round 40: Knit.

Round 41: *Knit 3, k2tog. Repeat from * around, end knit 2.

Cut MC and draw tail through remaining stitches. Knot and weave in all ends.

Variations

This piece is really 2 patterns in 1, so if your wee one is beyond the cocoon age, you could skip the cocoon and knit the cover-up pattern to your desired size to use as a blanket. Or if you just want to knit the cocoon, CO your 35 sts and take off! This little number would look just as fashionable knit in a muted color palette of rich earth tones — consider a combination of pumpkin, russet, and flax for autumn arrivals. Bernat *Bamboo* is an eco-friendly choice for one of the contrasting colors and provides a luxurious silky sheen. Just be sure to check your gauge when substituting yarns. Add a pom-pom or a tassel on the tootsies for a fun touch!

Other Yarns Shown

- 2 skeins Aslan Trends *Del Sur* in #1 White (87yd/80m - 3.5oz/100g; 100% merino wool) (MC)

- 1 skein Malabrigo *Merino Worsted* in #27 Bobby Blue (210yd/191m – 3.5oz/100g; 100% merino wool) (CC-1)

- 1 skein Farmhouse Yarns *Lumpy Bumpy* in Kaleidoscope (150yd/137m - 4oz/117g; 99% merino wool/1% nylon) (CC-2)

Your finished cocoon will look like a "T", with the rectangular cover-up portion at the top and the cocoon below.

RESOURCE DIRECTORY

If you'd like to track down the beautiful yarns (and needles!) mentioned in this book, here is a list of the company Web sites. Some are the manufacturers themselves, and some are larger online resources — all have lots to offer any knitter. Enjoy!

Alchemy Yarns of Transformation
alchemyyarns.com
(707) 823-3276

Araucania
knittingfever.com/c/araucania/yarn/

Artemis
Distributor of Hanah Silk
artemisinc.com
(888) 233-5187

Aslan Trends
aslantrends.com
(800) 314-8202

Bernat
bernat.com
(888) 368-8401

Berroco
berroco.com
(508) 278-2527

Be Sweet
besweetproducts.com
(415) 331-9676

Blue Sky Alpacas
blueskyalpacas.com
(888) 460-8862

Cascade Yarns
cascadeyarns.com
(206) 574-0040

Classic Elite Yarns
classiceliteyarns.com
(978) 453-2837

Colorful Nest Yarn Co.
colorfulnest.com

Debbie Bliss
debbieblissonline.com

Etsy
etsy.com

Farmhouse Yarns
farmhouseyarns.com
(860) 575-9050

Feza Yarns
fezayarns.com
(800) 684-3392

Judi & Co.
judiandco.com
(631) 499-8480

Katia
http://www.knittingfever.com/c/katia/yarn/

Kitchen Sink Dyeworks
kitchensinkdyeworks.com
(877) KSD-YARN

Knit Collage
knitcollage.com
(610) 999-5063

Knitting Help
knittinghelp.com

Lantern Moon
lanternmoon.com
(800) 530-4170

Lion Brand Yarn
lionbrand.com
(800) 258-YARN

Malabrigo Yarn
malabrigoyarn.com
(786) 866-6187

Ozark Handspun
ozarkhandspun.com
(573) 644-8736

Patons
patonsyarns.com

Ravelry
ravelry.com

Springtree Road
springtreeroad.com
(404) 931-3800

Spud & Chloë
spudandchloe.com
(888) 460-8862

Tahki Stacy Charles
tahkistacycharles.com
(800) 338-YARN

Trendsetter Yarns
trendsetteryarns.com
(800) 446-2425

TrickyKnits
trickyknits.com

WEBS
yarn.com
(800) FOR-WEBS

ACKNOWLEDGMENTS

This book is the result of an incredible amount of work and would not have been possible without the generous support of so many people.

To the many vendors who generously provided their beautiful yarns, ribbons, and needles for me to use in creating the designs for this book, I am so grateful for the faith you put in me. Thanks to Antonio Gonzalez-Arnao and Tobias Feder at Malabrigo Yarns; Angelo Fernandez and Dena Gonsieski at Aslan Trends; David Gentzsch at Ozark Handspun; Barry Klein, Myrna Klein, and Heidi Berger at Trendsetter Yarns; Debbi Skinner at Tahki Stacy Charles; Merri Fromm and Karen Rolstad at Blue Sky Alpacas; Donna Yacino at Berroco; Carol Martin at Farmhouse Yarns; Amy Small at Knit Collage; Judi Alweil and Sandy York at Judi & Co.; Brooke Long at Artemis Inc. (distributor of Hanah Silk Ribbons); Jeff Denecke and Susie Festa at Knitting Fever, Inc.; Kathy Elkins at WEBS; Austin and Gina Wilde at Alchemy Yarns of Transformation; Betsy Perry at Classic Elite Yarns; Shannon Dunbabin and Stacy Fletcher at Cascade Yarns; Nadine Curtis and Christine Carnal at Be Sweet; Ed and Wanda Jenkins at Jenkins Woodworking; Diana Youtsey at Lantern Moon; Amy Ross at Lion Brand; Howard Appell at Feza Yarns; Mercedes Tarasovich-Clark at Kitchen Sink Dyeworks; Sara Arblaster and Gord Moffat at Spinrite Yarns (for providing Bernat and Patons products); and Maya Henderson at Springtree Road. Thanks also to Tom and Maureen Turnbull at Turnbull Pottery for providing the lovely hand-thrown bowls used in some of the photos in this book; to my neighbors — Marshall Chapman and Chris Fletcher, and Kathy and Danny West — for opening your lovely homes and gardens to us for our photo shoots; and to Carolyn Smith and Marissa Harris at my local yarn store, Haus of Yarn. Each of you continually provided whatever I asked of you and have patiently waited to see the results. I hope you are pleased with this book.

To the parents of the sweet babies featured here — I hope you find those long days of photo shoots well worth it! You were all a delight and I thank you for sharing the first few days of your babies' lives with us.

To the talented Brooke Kelly, a true baby whisperer whose tireless hours behind the camera and in her editing studio brought my designs to life and made this pattern book a collection of beautiful images. You have been an absolutely delightful partner on this project and I look forward to working with you again. Lucky for me you live in Nashville!

Very special thanks to Robin Haywood, publishing director at Sellers Publishing, who called me out of the blue one day and took a chance on turning this knitter into a first-time author. I am so grateful to you for giving me this amazing opportunity to shine. I also extend a thank-you to Mary Baldwin for the production work, and for your patience in making every change I requested (right down to the last minute!). I am proud of our efforts and hope you are too.

I want to especially thank my editor, Cary Hull, who tumbled into my life at the beginning of this journey and has guided me every step of the way. I didn't know how much I needed you until you arrived. Very simply, I could never have done this without you.

And to my dedicated gang of dear friends and test-knitters — Pamela Roller, Margaret Hartge, Elisabeth Green, and Kim Gardner — thank you for all those endless hours of knitting these pieces over and over again! I hope it's all right to pay you in yarn.

And last, but not least, thank you to my devoted husband, Timothy, and our seven children for patiently waiting . . . and waiting . . . for this book to be finished.

INDEX

Welcome home, little one.

Welcoming Home Baby the Handcrafted Way is a collection of 20 creative patterns designed to celebrate the arrival of a newborn. Fun and quick to knit, these designs showcase Tricia Drake's (of TrickyKnits.com) signature style of using soft, bulky yarns knit on unexpectedly big needles to create truly unusual pieces to welcome your wee one. You'll find a chunky new spin on classic designs like the Twisted Taffy Hat, whimsical confections such as the Birthday Wrap to herald a new addition, toasty pieces like the Eskimo Kiss Hooded Cocoon for snuggling, and the cozy Peek-a-Boo Pod for tender newborn photographs.

What the Press Is Saying:

"The greatest innovation Drake makes in designs for babies is using thick, bulky yarns on large knitting needles. These yarns change not only the look and feel of the garments she's designed, but they also shorten the time it takes to knit them. There's no skimping on the cuteness factor in any of the projects."
— *Foreword reviews, May 2011*

"Some of the designs in this book are so unique and so perfect for a new baby that they seem commissioned by Mother Nature herself. If there is one sentence that could describe this book it is: Tricia's designs are from the baby's point of view."
— *Living Crafts magazine, March 2011*

"In her cute and cuddly book, Tricia Drake, turns conventional baby knitting on it's head by creating wee knits with big yarns."
— *KnitPurlGirl.com, March 2011*

"The results appear deliciously complex, yet the designs are relatively straight-forward. Set apart from most baby knits by the use of large needles (nothing under size 10 and mostly size 15, 17, and 19) and chunky yarns, this scale works surprisingly well for tiny babies."
— *Publishers Weekly, March 2011*

Twisted Taffy Hat

Eskimo Kiss Hooded Cocoon

Ribbons & Bows Cocoon

Birthday Wrap Blanket

Peek-a-Boo Pod

SELLERS PUBLISHING

7009
$18.95

U.S. $18.95 / CAN. $21.95
ISBN-13: 978-1-4162-0627-9
51895

9 781416 206279

WELCOMING HOME BABY

the Handcrafted Way

Published by Sellers Publishing, Inc.

Text and patterns © 2011 Tricia Drake

Photography © 2011 Brooke Kelly,
except where noted, photography © 2011 Gina Bilyeu:
pp. 9, 32, 33, 35, 37, 60, 62, 63, 90, 91, 93, 98, 99, 105, 106

Sellers Publishing, Inc.
161 John Roberts Road, South Portland, Maine 04106
Visit our Web site: www.sellerspublishing.com • E-mail: rsp@rsvp.com

ISBN: 13: 978-1-4162-0627-9
e-ISBN: 978-1-4162-0747-4

Library of Congress Control Number: 2010934292

10 9 8 7 6 5 4 3

Printed and bound in China

Visit www.trickyknits.com or www.sellerspublishing.com for the most
recent Errata Sheet, which includes revisions, notes from the author, and
suggestions for yarn substitutions. Yarn, needles, and customized kits for
many of these projects are available at www.trickyknits.com.